brenna maloney

sockology

16 NEW SOCK CREATURES • CUTE & CUDDLY...WEIRD & WILD

stashBOOKS.

an imprint of C&T Publishing

Text, photography, and artwork copyright © 2011 by Brenna Maloney
Photography and artwork copyright © 2011 by C&T Publishing, Inc.

Publisher: Amy Marson

Creative Director: Gailen Runge

Acquisitions Editor: Susanne Woods

Editor: Cynthia Bix

Technical Editor: Gailen Runge

Cover/Book Designer: Kristen Yenche

Production Coordinator: Zinnia Heinzmann

Production Editor: Julia Cianci

Illustrator: Brenna Maloney

Photography by Chuck Kennedy

Published by Stash Books, an imprint of C&T Publishing, Inc.,
P.O. Box 1456, Lafayette, CA 94549

Library of Congress
Cataloging-in-Publication Data
Maloney, Brenna.
 Sockology : 16 new sock creatures, cute & cuddly--
weird & wild / Brenna Maloney.
    p. cm.
 Sequel to: Socks Appeal.
 ISBN 978-1-60705-407-8 (soft cover)
 1. Soft toy making. 2. Socks. I. Maloney, Brenna.
Socks Appeal.II. Title.
 TT174.3.M362 2010
 745.592'43--dc22
                                    2010051958

Printed in China

10 9 8 7 6 5 4 3 2 1

contents

acknowledgments

I have two remarkable teams that helped me create this book. The folks at C&T Publishing have once again been phenomenal every step of the way. I could not ask for a better professional partner. A special nod goes to my editor, Cynthia Bix. Any woman who can see the humor in "squirrel underpants" is a woman I want in my corner.

My other team is built from my family. I'm grateful to my husband, who endured countless hours of silliness with me as he shot the fantastic photographs for this book. My parents and my sister showed unending support—from sending me socks, to letting me talk through "design flaws," to staying calm and reassuring when my hair was on fire and I was in pants-wetting mode (sadly, a common occurrence). And to my sons. So much of this book is for you and because of you. I will always consider myself lucky to be your mom.

sockology 101

I thought I had gotten all this sock stuff out of my system with my first book, *Socks Appeal*. And I was okay for a while. Really. But one day, I found myself making a crocodile. I didn't intend to do it. It was an accident. Well, sort of.

Next it was the kangaroo and joey. "You're doing it again, aren't you?" my husband asked, nervously looking on. "No, no, I'm not doing anything," I answered defensively. By the time I started work on the rooster, the jig was up. "You're working on another book, aren't you?" he demanded. Well… maybe?

Some things can't be helped, I guess.

Recently, my mother confessed to me that she found it hard *to cut up a sock*. My mother, who is brave in all things. My mother, who is a creative genius. Myself, I've cut up so many socks by now that I don't even think about it. I don't even buy socks with the intention of wearing them anymore. When I see a sock in a store, chances are I've mentally dissected it before I've made it to the checkout line.

It didn't take long for my mother to get over her aversion to cutting up socks. But her comment made me realize that I was probably adopted after being abandoned as an infant by circus folk. No. No, that's not what it made me realize. It made me realize that her reaction is perfectly normal. It *is* a little weird to cut up your socks. If you are feeling this, too, I'm going to have to ask you to tough it out. You're playing with the big boys now. This ain't no beginner's book.

Well, that's not exactly true. To be honest, you don't need that much skill to make these projects. What you will need is courage. Not only am I going to ask you to whip out those scissors, but I'm also I'm going to ask you to drop a few of those inhibitions. No, no, I'm not talking about sewing in the nude. Good grief! No one needs to see *that*. I'm talking about really throwing yourself into these creations and making them uniquely yours. I will give you guidelines. I will give you as much help as you need. But I want you to feel free to ignore me, too. I want you to size these patterns up and say, "Well, I might take this in a different direction." Make it yours. *Own it.*

It comes down to this: We all have demands on our time. We've got X to do and Y to do and X to do again. If you're willing to sit down with me for an hour, let's really *do* this thing, okay? I'm ready. Are you? Take a deep breath. Let's go!

tools of the trade: socks

For the projects in this book, we won't be using every type of sock under the rainbow. We will be using a lot of knee-highs and maybe even a pair of tights. We will need our fair share of crew socks—fancy ones like angora and metallic crew socks—which will bring a lot of richness to the things we make.

There will be plenty of room for oddities, like our friend the creepy toe sock. Of course, toe socks must be slated for sewing because no one in their right mind can stand wearing them and having their toes separated into individual compartments. It's just not natural.

And we should discuss the anklet. I want to be clear on my position. Anklets, as a sock style, are a bad idea. What is the point? Once you put your shoe on, you can't even tell the sock is there. It's a waste.

Anklets, as a raw material for sewing, however, are brilliant! Oh, yes. Yes, you should use them just as often as you can. They come in all sorts of fabulous colors and patterns. And it honestly is their express wish to be used for a greater purpose.

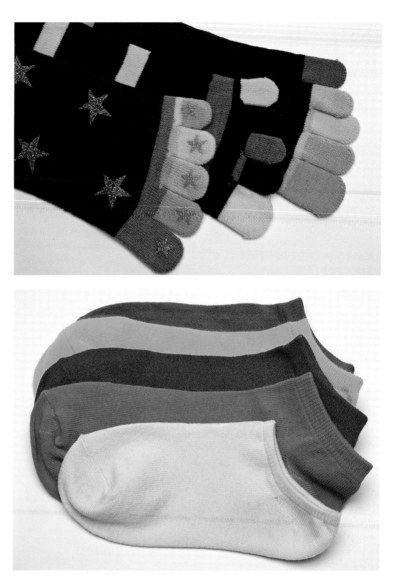

I think anklets feel this longing more strongly than cuffed socks. *Those* socks get respect in the sock world. Not so the lowly anklet. Yet anklets do not wish to be trod on. They wish, like so many of us, to have a higher calling. Think of it this way: Would you rather be worn on a person's foot or made into something artistic? Hmm…tough call there. And so, knowing this, we really must acknowledge our moral imperative to free the anklet as often as we can from the Oppression of the Foot. I plan to do my part, anyway.

the triple S

In my first book, *Socks Appeal*—a truly gripping book, by the way—I gave you a piece of advice: Never, ever throw away single socks or your unused sock bits. All the little pieces—heels and toes and cuffs—that you cut off and didn't need? I told you to keep them, remember? If you followed my advice, and I'm sure you did, you should have a pretty decent Triple S by now—Sock Scrap Stash. This is one of those tongue twisters, you know, like, "How much wood would a woodchuck chuck if a woodchuck could chuck wood?" It's simply impossible to say out loud—Sock Scrap Stash—but the alliteration was just too hard to resist, and I had to call it something. "Crazy Lady's Bulging Bag of Sock Bits" was so much less appealing.

Wait. You say you don't have a Triple S yet? No worries. If you're joining us now and didn't suffer through the last set of patterns with me, all is not lost. It's never too late to start, and in the meantime I'll just direct you to cut up more anklets!

Now that I think about it, I probably should have added a fourth S, for "Secret." If you're like me, and you probably are, you don't want to go advertising to your loved ones how large your stash is. Trust me. I've learned this one the hard way. If they get one look at that overflowing basket of sock scraps, they'll reach for the commitment papers for you to sign. So, you might just want to keep that under your hat. You and I know you have one. And I'm not telling.

Your Triple S (or large collection of anklets) is going to come in handy for this book. For a lot of these patterns, we're only going to need a little. A flash of red here. A hint of pink there. Just scraps, really. So, having a scrap stash handy will be, well, handy.

other materials

STUFF IT

My go-to item for stuffing sock animals has traditionally been polyfill—any brand. But in this book, we're going to go beyond that. For a few of the patterns, I'm going to ask you to use rice. I don't care what kind. If you prefer jasmine or basmati, it makes no nevermind to me. But you'll see a remarkable difference in how rice—whatever kind—can shape and give character to your creature. And if for some reason it doesn't work out, you can always cook it for a little snack later.

BLING IT

You'll need some fairly standard decorative bits and pieces—ribbon, beaded trim, and DMC floss for manes and faces.

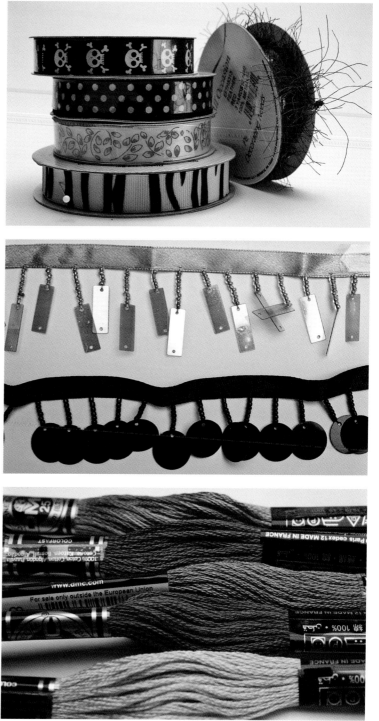

For eyes, you'll need buttons—regular ones and any interesting novelty ones you run across—and, God help me, black seed beads.

You'll soon see that I favor seed beads, viewing them as the perfect eyes for most sock creatures. It's very tiresome of me to use them so often, so when I direct you to use them, feel free to ignore me. I will in no way be offended.

ZING IT

I *am* going to ask you to use a lot of weird things. You'll need empty wooden spools for some projects.

You'll need broken watch parts or compasses or odd bits of plastic for other projects.

I might even ask you to smash open an old calculator or cell phone and raid it for parts.

Oh, yeah. Be warned. Things are about to get pretty weird in the world of socks....

Rules of Engagement

Now, I hope you don't think I'm going to make this easy on you. No, no, of course not. You're going to have to follow some *rules*.

- Turn socks inside out when you cut and stitch the body parts together.

- Always leave a gap of $1/2''$ to $1''$ (1.25 cm to 2.5 cm) when you stitch the body, so you can turn it right side out before stuffing.

- Stuff fully, but don't pack too tight (unless I tell you to).

- Use a slip stitch (Stitch Gallery, page 14) to close up the gap after stuffing.

- To hand stitch limbs and other parts to your beasties' bodies, fold under the raw edge and use a slip stitch.

- Try to maintain a $1/4''$ (.5 cm) seam allowance on most of these projects, if possible.

- Keep the swearing to a minimum, especially in the presence of children.

By the way, I use my trusty Kenmore sewing machine, but you can sew everything by hand if you like.

POKERS

And a few words about an important tool you'll need: a poker. You might need more than one. I have a couple I turn to when I need to turn something. Alex Anderson's 4-in-1 Essential Sewing Tool (left, available from C&T Publishing) is a fine tool to have in your arsenal. If you don't want to get too fancy, I recommend the pencil (right) or, my secret favorite, the kebab stick (middle).

Having the right tool is important, but so is knowing how to use it. I'll be honest with you: We're going to be doing an awful lot of turning in this book, and some of the things we will be turning will be very, very narrow and it will make you want to say bad words. However, proper technique can help cut down on frustrations and ruined socks. Here—let me give you an example.

You're in the middle of turning frog feet, when suddenly there's a blockage and you can't get through. What do you do with that kebab stick?

Jab jab jabbity jab jab jabbity jabbity jabbity JAB JAB JAB POKE! Awwwwwww....!@#$!v@#$v !@#$.

Right.

Let's replay the videotape. Here's what went wrong: You rushed the job. You got frustrated. You overpoked. It happens. Don't beat yourself up. Let's run through it again with a few tips:

Jab. Jab.

At the first sign of trouble, you need to step away from the kebab stick. Take a little break. Go for a walk. Admire your sleeping children. Pet an animal.

Jab. Jab. Jab.

Go to your happy place.

Jab. Jab. Jab.

Eat some Junior Mints.

Jab.

Voilà! Done!

See?

Basic hand stitches used in these projects

Backstitch

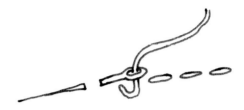

Running stitch

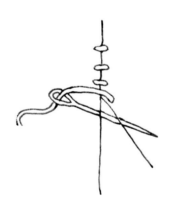

Slip stitch

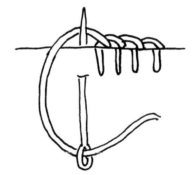

Blanket stitch

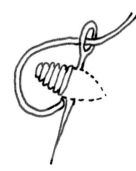

Satin stitch

patterns

I seem to be pattern-happy in this book. Sorry about that. Eight of these projects have patterns—hand drawn by yours truly, I'm afraid. You can use them or not. I keep pleading with my publisher to hire someone who actually knows how to draw, but no dice. I guess my publisher thinks that if you're going to be subjected to my weird directions, you might as well suffer my bad art as well.

You can just photocopy the patterns (they're full-size) and trace them onto your socks. Folks can get fairly particular about what they use to trace a pattern. I will avert my eyes while you select your weapon of choice—be it marking pen, chalk, pencil, or toothpaste.

pratfalls and predicaments

Now, in this book I am trying to encourage you to be brave and *try* stuff. In trying stuff, however, you run the risk of three outcomes:

1. Frustrating yourself

2. Producing something hideous

3. Producing something genius

Right. I know what you're thinking: I want what's behind Door Number 3. Believe me, we *all* do. But the reality is, you and I are probably going to make a lot of crap along the way. We're going to make mistakes. Some will be fixable, others—not so much. Just to prove to you that this happens to *everyone*, I'm going to show you some of my dismal failures.

Yeah, I know. I'm going out on a limb here. If you see some of my flops, you might get a real sense of what an idiot I am. I'm going to take that risk, though, because I really do think this is important. If for nothing else, to give you a good laugh.

GOOD IDEA, BAD EXECUTION

A friend of mine suggested I make a hedgehog. What a splendid idea, I thought. What's not to love? They are cute. Except when they are made by me. Just look at this thing! I know. It hurts. Okay, avert your eyes. Just take quick glances at it and then turn away. I don't want to induce blindness here.

What happened? Well, I don't really know. I chose a good sock, a lovely tan angora. His size and shape are okay. But ye gods, what have I done to his prickles? I used DMC floss. Little tassels of it. Maybe I need more? A lot more? Because he looks so… so…well, bald…and horrible.

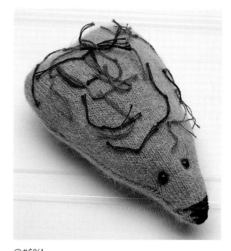

@#$%!

GOOD IDEA, MAYBE NOT

My older son drew a fantastic little line drawing one day, prized by me for its utter simplicity. He called it "Captain Marble," which made me like it even more for its absurdity. Here again, what's not to like? He's a "captain," after all. And a marble to boot. And he's wearing an eye patch. Anything looks more interesting when it's wearing an eye patch. This little dude is even brandishing a sword! So, I made him. And here he sits. (For the record, my son really likes him.)

It's all part of the creative process. Some days, you sit down and you're a freakin' genius. Other days, you sit down and you create a balding hedgehog. Fight the good fight. Keep trying.

things that fly...

Designed and made by Brenna Maloney.

duck

Finished size: About 3″ (7.5 cm) tall

I'm going to give you something very special here—a duck without wings *or* feet. A *sitting* duck. Pretty funny, huh? A flightless bird in a chapter called "Things That Fly." What gives? Oh, I'm just messing with you a little. Why do you need a sitting duck? Well, if you've had as many bad bosses as I have, you'll like having a sitting duck on your desk at work. When the going gets tough, Duck ain't goin' nowhere. But at least you can be sitting ducks together.

instructions

1. Here's our first chance to use some anklets. Woo hoo! Find yourself a colorful pair to convert into Duck. You will also need to raid your Triple S (Sock Scrap Stash, page 9) to find a small bit of contrasting sock for his beak.

2. Normally I would advise you to "wing it" and just cut everything away from the sock that doesn't look like a duck. But as Duck is the first pattern in this book, it seems a bit unfair to put so much pressure on you. So instead, I've actually drawn a pattern for you to use (page 23). You'll find the pattern for Duck's side body and another odd bit. The word for this odd bit is, technically, "gusset." But for the purpose of this book, we shall use the more technical term, "Duck belly."

3. Now then, be so kind as to turn your anklets inside out and trace these patterns onto the socks. You will need 2 side bodies but only 1 Duck belly.

4. Cut out the pieces. Don't forget that little contrasting bit from your Triple S. Cut off 2 rectangular pieces large enough for a beak.

5. Place 1 beak piece on 1 of the side body pieces, right sides together, and stitch them together straight across Duck's nose. Do the same with the other side body and beak pieces.

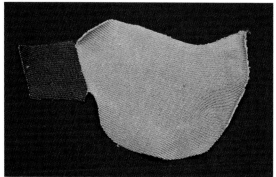

6. Place the side bodies right sides together, and, starting at Duck's butt, sew along his back toward his beak. When you get to the beak, free-sew a triangle and trim off the excess about ¼" (.5 cm) from the stitching line.

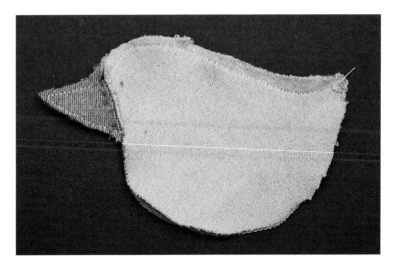

7. You'll need the Duck belly segment now. Line it up at the butt. I've marked the pattern pieces so you can line up points B and C at Duck's butt with points B and C on Duck's belly. With right sides together, pin and sew, easing the pieces together along 1 side.

8. Sew up the remaining side, but leave open a small gap—maybe ½" (1.25 cm)—so you can turn Duck.

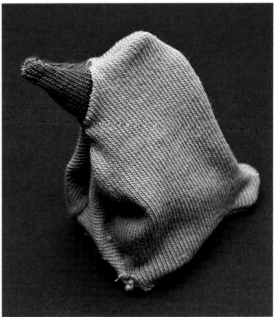

9. Turn Duck. Okay. He looks a little on the pathetic side. But wait. Here's where it gets good. Go to your kitchen. Yes, you're looking a little weak. You might need a snack. You were hoping this would be an easy pattern, and already I've used the word "gusset" on you. While you're getting your snack, rustle up a bag of rice to stuff Duck. While you're in the kitchen, also snag a funnel. Then return to your Duck husk.

10. Gently pour some rice into the opening in Duck's side. Use the funnel to guide the rice into Duck. Don't do any heavy drinking before attempting this or your aim will be off. (I guess I should have told you that when you were in the kitchen.) Don't pack him too tightly. When he's had enough, stitch up the hole in his side by hand with a needle and matching thread. Use a slip stitch to hide your work (see Stitch Gallery, page 14).

11. You're nearly there, but for Pete's sake, please give him some eyes. Isn't it bad enough that he doesn't have feet or wings? He should at least be able to *see* when your bad boss is coming. Tiny black seed beads should do the trick.

You'll have fun making more sitting ducks. Go ahead. Litter your desk with them. The brighter and more cheerful the colors, the better. That way, you'll be giving the anklet something useful to do *and* giving yourself plenty of company to take on the boss.

Don't Be Alarmed If Your Sitting Ducks Congregate

They like to gossip about office politics.

Duck water cooler talk: "I like birdseed." "Yeah." "Yeah, birdseed."

"Is this the line for the copier?"

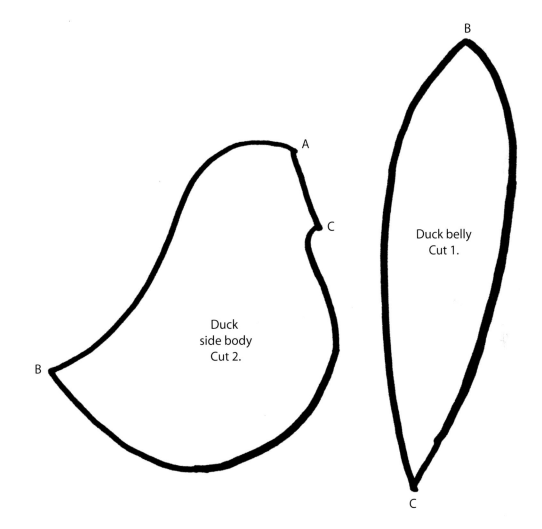

A

C

Duck belly
Cut 1.

Duck
side body
Cut 2.

B

B

C

Designed and made by Brenna Maloney.

bee

Finished size: About 3″ (7.5 cm) long

Most of us spend large parts of our lives toiling away at "the day job." That might be a full load of stay-at-home responsibilities or a full-time job out in the cold, cruel world. Either way, we have to be productive bees and get our work done. Today, we're going to channel the productive powers of our inner worker bee by making a little sock bee.

instructions

1. There are 2 methods for making the Bee. I'm going to give a nod to the traditionalists and show you how to make a black and yellow Bee. For that, you'll need to scrounge up a yellow and a black sock. I've used anklets. Naturally. (To make a simpler, pre-striped version in different colors, see page 29.)

2. Cut off the heels and toes of each sock. For this pattern, you're mostly interested in those middle bits, which are now tubes.

3. Cut open both tubes, and lay the socks out flat.

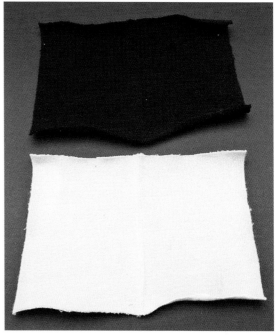

4. We need to create a few black and yellow strips for Mr. Bee's body. So, with right sides together, stitch the black and yellow blocks together across the top.

5. Trim about ½" (1.25 cm) away from the stitching to make a yellow and black strip, and open it flat. Save the black and yellow pieces that you cut away; we'll use them later.

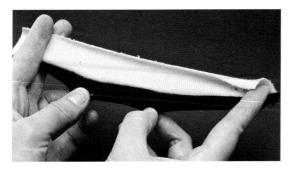

6. Set this aside, and go back to the black sock toe section that you cut off earlier. Turn the toe inside out, and free-sew 2 little wings. Just eyeball them to make them "wing shaped."

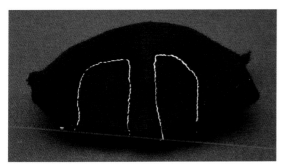

7. Trim away the excess and turn the wings. Very nice. I see that you understood me perfectly when I said, "wing shaped."

8. Now go back to the yellow and black strip, and pin the wings to it as shown. We want to sew the wings into the next strip.

9. Take the yellow piece left over from Step 5, and pin it to the black side of the yellow and black strip, right sides together, with the wings in between.

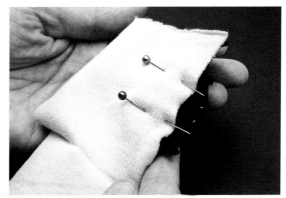

10. Sew them together, and open flat. See how Bee's wings look now? You can trim off some of the yellow strip's width before continuing.

11. The leftover black piece from Step 5 will be the final strip. Sew it to the yellow side of the strip set. Trim it a little wider than the other strips because it will be Bee's stinger. If you are keeping score, you should now have a set of 4 strips sewn together: yellow–black/wings–yellow–black.

12. Now fold down an end of the strip set with the fold between the 2 wings. You might want to pin it in place so it doesn't slide.

13. Starting at the yellow head end, sew yourself a bee shape. Ha! I know. That's not very helpful-sounding advice, but it's really not too hard. Just sew *very* slowly. Bee's head should be rounded. His tum should be fat. As you come up to the back end, sew straight up to a point to give him his stinger. *Do not forget* to leave a little open space in the middle, near his tum. You'll need this hole for turning. You don't know how many bees I've made where I've completely stitched the darn thing up.

14. Carefully trim the seam allowances.

15. Turn Bee. You may need to use a pencil or, better yet, a kebab stick to help you turn him.

16. Stuff him firmly with polyfill. Slipstitch the open gap closed, using a needle and black thread.

17. Mr. Bee would like a set of eyes, please. I recommend tiny black seed beads for his tiny head. Be sure to sew them on the yellow part of his head so that they can be seen.

18. Using 2 or 3 strands of black DMC embroidery thread, backstitch a smile on his face.

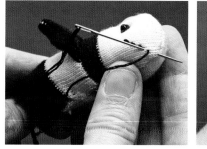

19. He needs some antennae; so rustle up some black craft wire and cutters. Cut off a 4" (10 cm) segment. Slide it through his head above his eyes. Owwwww! Use a pencil or your trusty kebab stick to curl the ends of the wire. Bzzzzzzz!

20. If you want to give Bee some feet, find a black pipe cleaner. Cut off a 3" (7.5 cm) segment, and shape it like a U. Bend the ends up to form feet. Make 2 of these, and tack them on Bee's underside with black thread.

He's ready!

Bee #2

I did tell you there's another way.
Instead of sewing separate bands of
color, find a sock with stripes. Most
of your work is already done, then.
Just follow Steps 2 and 3, make
a small cut to insert the wings,
and finish up as for the black and
yellow version from Step 12.

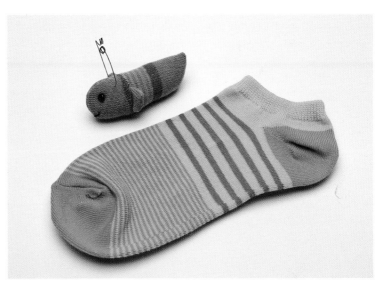

"Passing on the right, mate."

"Uh . . . I think you have some pollen on your nose."

Designed and made by Brenna Maloney.

rooster

Finished size: Body about 6″ (15.25 cm) tall, plus 6″ (15.25 cm) for comb and legs

Yes, roosters *can too* fly! They *do* belong in this chapter. Not that they go on long flights or anything. They've got nothing on the albatross, maybe, but how do you think they get to the top of the fence post or the farmhouse or wherever they go when they need to wake up the world? Yes, yes, I'm well aware that the sock version of Rooster is as flat a pancake. So, okay, *this rooster* won't be doing any flying, but he's fun to make, just the same.

instructions

1. Anybody got a toe sock? You'll need a pair of long knee-high toe socks and a solid anklet. The toe sock should have as many colors as possible. If you don't have a suitable anklet, just go through your Triple S and look for some orange or yellow scraps.

2. We're going to do a little cutting now. On the first sock, snip off the toe section. With what's left, cut 2 pieces, 1 slightly longer than the other. On the second sock, cut out a piece to match the first shorter piece. All the other socks bits can be set aside for your Triple S.

3. You can try your hand at cutting out a rooster shape freehand from the longer segment of the first sock. Or, you can trace the pattern (page 36) and use it to cut out the body. Once you've got Rooster's body cut out, place the cut toe section—the comb—above his head and take a look. Does it need a little trimming, or does one of the end toes need lopping off? You might have to do a little surgery here to make sure the toes are going to fit on the head to make a proper comb.

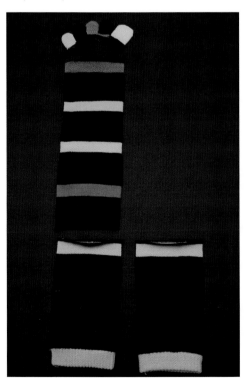

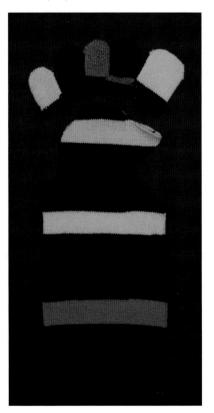

4. Now I'm going to ask you to chop off his beak. I know, I know. It's a bit distressing. But we're about to give him a better beak, so it's okay. I promise he won't even feel it.

5. For a replacement beak, cut a little 2-layer section from the heel of the anklet, and separate the layers. On each half of Rooster's body, sew on a replacement piece straight across the new beak's wide end.

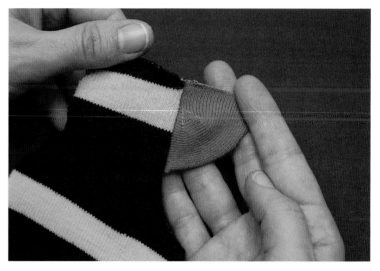

6. With his body right sides together, sew all around the new beak in a triangle, and trim the seam allowances. Don't sew the top of his head yet, though. That's our next step.

7. Tuck that comb in place, sandwiched between the front and back body pieces, matching the raw edges. The sock toes should face inward; pin, pin, pin to hold it in place.

8. Sew from a shoulder, across the comb, to the top of the beak. Then pick up again at the bottom of the beak, and sew down to the shoulder.

9. Let's move on to the wings. Earlier, you cut 2 sections near the sock cuffs. Turn both sections inside out, and free-sew the wings. You want the wings to look a bit wavy, to imply feathers. If you are using a striped sock, step down the wing with each color band change. I made it impossible to see the thread line in the example, so my editor added a helpful red line to the photo.

10. Trim the seam allowances, and turn both wings. Work the "feathered" ends with your fingers to make sure they turn all the way and are flat.

11. Turn Rooster's body inside out again. Sandwich the wings between the front and back body, just below the shoulders and pointing in toward the chest. Stitch along both sides of the body to trap both wings. Keep the bottom open.

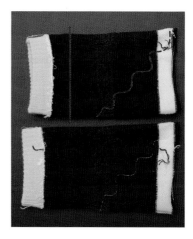

12. You should now have an odd-looking bundle, like this. You can turn Rooster to check and see that everything is looking good. Then turn him back one last time, if you will.

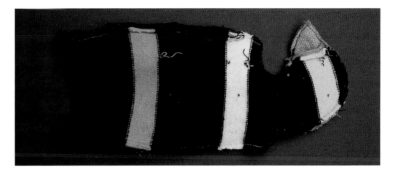

13. We're nearly there, but Rooster needs some legs. Turn the anklet inside out and free-sew 2 spindly little rooster legs. This is not as hard as it sounds. You want a skinny leg part (about 1" (2.5 cm) to 1½" (3.75 cm) long) and some toes on each foot. How many? I don't really care. I've given mine 3. But if one foot has 3 toes, the other one should, too. Otherwise, you'll need to make up a pretty good story about how Rooster lost a toe. Sew very slowly. My rooster's legs and feet are pretty uneven and ridiculous looking, but I think that's part of their charm (she says nervously).

14. Trim the seam allowances, and turn the legs. This will be a nightmare, as you can imagine. Just work slowly, use your kebab stick, and try not to swear like a sailor.

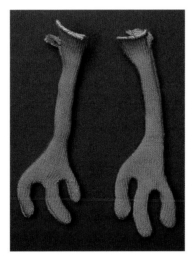

15. Insert the legs into the bottom body opening, with the toes pointing toward the head. You don't need to center the legs unless you are obsessive-compulsive about symmetry. If you are, then center them by all means. I'll not get in the way of that. I don't have that particular issue, so I like putting my legs off to one side a bit.

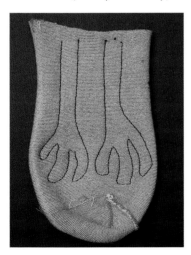

16. Stitch across Rooster's bottom, trapping the legs. Remember to leave a small opening so you can turn him one last time.

17. If all went well, Rooster should now have all his parts firmly stitched into place. Let's stuff him with polyfill. Not too much, here. We want to keep him relatively flat. Don't forget to stitch closed the small opening you left for stuffing. We don't want the old boy's innards falling out.

18. Choose whatever sort of eye you like. I've had luck with seed beads, but also with large, wild buttons. Give him something decent to crow about!

As you become practiced with Rooster, you'll have fun making him a little more irregular. You won't need a pattern for his body, and you'll be tempted to pick crazy eyes for him. I tend to think things look a little better when they look half crazy anyway. I mean, c'mon, have you ever seen a real rooster? Those things can look a little rough. It makes sense—getting up that early in the morning. On purpose. No wonder they spend the rest of the day bossing the hens around. They're cranky.

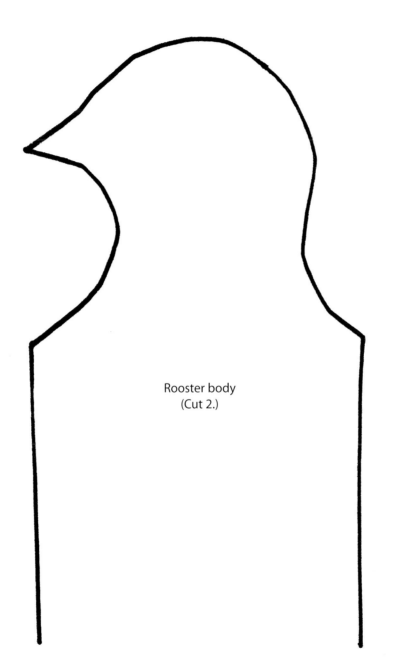

Rooster body
(Cut 2.)

...and things that don't

Designed and made by Brenna Maloney.

fox

Finished size: About 4″ (10 cm) wide and 10″ (25.5 cm) high, depending on how long you make those legs.

I was working on this fox pattern when I said to my husband, "It *would* be great if George Clooney paid off our mortgage!" Now, my husband has gotten used to these strange mental outbursts of mine. But even he was surprised by this one. "*Where* did that come from?" he asked. *Well...*

Foxes, of course, made me think of "The Fantastic Mr. Fox," a story by Roald Dahl that was made into an animated film. George Clooney did the voiceover for Mr. Fox. What you might not know is that I would be perfect for George Clooney, if only we could meet. I am quite certain that one glance at me sitting here in the wee hours of the night typing—my middle-aged, lumpy self, clad in my rocket pajamas, hair all akimbo—well, such a vision of loveliness would quite overwhelm him. He would say, "Good God, woman! I must have you!" But I, virtuous soul that I am, would politely decline. And he, who surely must be as chivalrous and wonderful as we all suppose, would respect my decision not to run away with him and live in his Italian villa. But he would say to himself, "A woman like that deserves to have her mortgage paid."

Well, anyway, back to the fox at hand...

instructions

1. For this fox, a pair of crew socks should do the trick. I chose angora because they are so soft. I was hoping for a nice foxy orange or red, but, alas, none could be found in my sock collection. So I had to go with this very unnatural blue. You will also use a third angora sock, white, for Fox's paws, nose tip, ears, and tail tip (or use something from your Triple S).

2. To start, you'll just need to work with 1 blue sock and the white sock. (The other blue sock you can ball up in a little pile for later.) Snip off the stubby little cuffs on both socks. From the blue sock, cut 1 segment about 4" (10 cm) long and another about 1" (2.5 cm) long. Cut off the heel so that you can cut another piece about 3" (7.5 cm) long. Snip off the toe. From the white sock, cut 2 segments, each 1" (2.5 cm) wide.

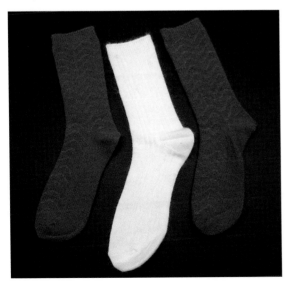

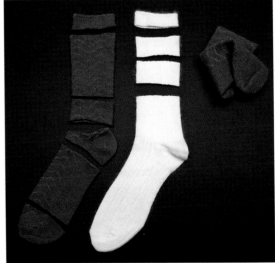

3. Cut open 1 side of a 1" (2.5 cm) segment from each sock to make a long strip, and cut each strip in half crosswise.

4. Place a blue and a white strip right sides together, and free-sew 2 pointy fox ears, leaving the bottoms of the ears open.

5. Trim away the excess, and turn the ears. The white sides will be the fronts.

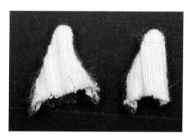

6. To make Fox's legs, cut open 1 side of the 3" (7.5 cm) segment you cut from the blue sock and the 1" (2.5 cm) segment from the white sock. Place them right sides together, and stitch across the top.

7. Fold this piece in half lengthwise, and free-sew 4 skinny little legs. Make 2 extra-long shapes for the back legs, and 2 shorter shapes for the front legs.

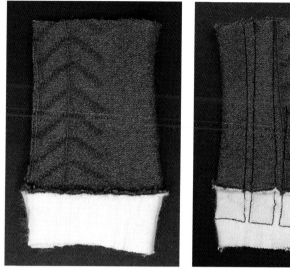

8. Trim away the excess, and gently turn. Set these pieces aside for now.

9. Go back to the second blue sock—the one I told you to ball up and forget about. Well, okay, that was harsh of me because now we need the dang thing. Go and get it. I'll wait.

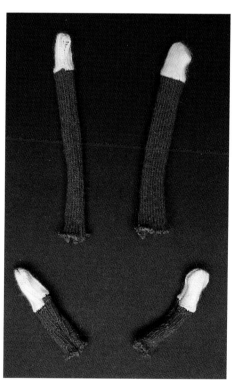

10. Thank you. Now then, with this sock and what's left of the white sock, we'll give our Fox a head and a tail. On the blue sock, snip off the cuff and cut off the foot section. On the white sock, cut 2 more 1″ (2.5 cm) segments.

11. Cut the blue segment in half to make 2 shorter segments, cut open 1 side of each, and lay flat. Cut open 1 side of both white segments as well. You are going to sew a white strip to each of the blue pieces, just as you did in Step 6.

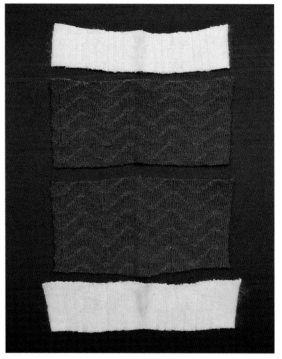

12. Fold 1 piece in half and free-sew a tail. You know what fox tails look like, right? They're very bushy, with a white tip. Be sure to leave the base of the tail open to turn it.

13. From the other segment, we're going to make Fox's head. Fold the piece in half and insert the 2 ears at the top, or blue, end. The ears should be pointing downward, toward the white band (which will be the nose). Pin the ears in place to keep them from shifting while you sew.

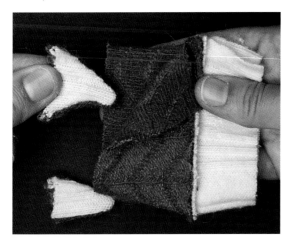

14. Free-sew a wide triangle, trapping the ears. Make sure to leave a small opening on 1 side for turning.

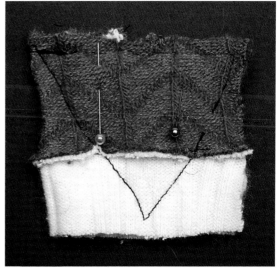

15. Go ahead and turn. Isn't Fox wonderful? I love his pointed little head and his pointed little ears.

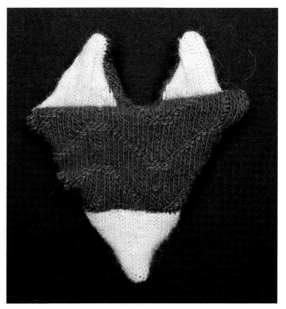

16. Remember that 4" (10 cm) segment I asked you to cut from the first blue sock? Well, that's going to be Fox's body. Slice open one of the open sides. By now you've turned the tail (not to be confused with turning tail and running…running…running far away from this pattern). Place the tail right below the fold of the 4" (10 cm) segment.

17. At the bottom of Fox's body, place his 2 long legs, pointing upward.

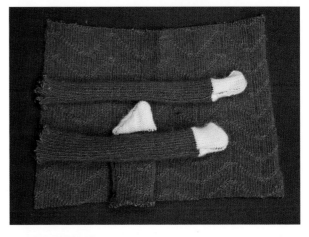

18. Fold the body in half again, with right sides together. You'll have to squeeze and mash everything in place. And then go ahead and pin, pin, pin to keep things from sliding while you sew. It's like a little sandwich now.

19. Stitch all the way around—leaving a small opening for turning. You're locking in Fox's tail and back legs. Turn his body. Boy does *that* look weird. Do I even know what I am doing? Yes, yes, I do. Don't worry. Go ahead and stuff his body. Not too much. He needs to be a little on the flat side. Stitch closed the small opening you left for turning.

20. Hand stitch his *wittle* front paws in place. One goes on top of the body and the other goes slightly underneath.

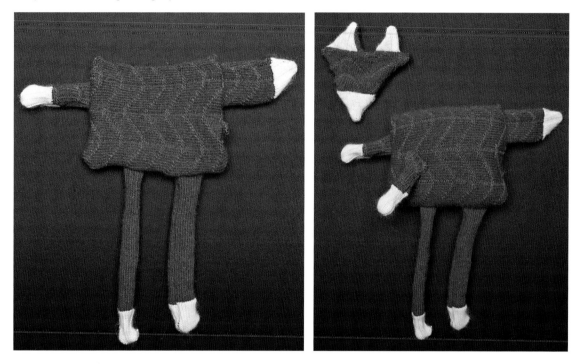

21. Attach Fox's flat head to the corner of his body, between his little arms.

22. Give him some eyes. You know I used black seed beads because, well, I can't seem to stop myself from doing that.

23. For whiskers, use heavy-duty black thread. Run a section through the tip of the nose, and then run it right back. Cut, then knot, the ends at the base of the nose so that Fox's new whiskers are locked into place.

He's fabulous. Even George Clooney would approve.

Designed and made by Brenna Maloney.

monkey

Finished size: About 7″ (18 cm) tall

Why is it that whenever we see an image of a monkey, it's joyous? Have you ever noticed that? I'm not complaining. My younger son drew a monkey for me and that monkey is a beaming, happy little thing. Have you ever seen a sad monkey? No. Well, okay. Once. In H.A. Rey's *Curious George Plays in the Snow*, when Curious George loses the bunny he took out of the bunny hutch. It's less of a sad-monkey face and more of a shame-monkey face. Probably because he knows the Man with the Yellow Hat is going to kick his monkey butt for getting into trouble again. But still. My point is…what was my point? Oh, yeah, my point is, monkeys are often depicted as joyous creatures—and I for one am not going to stand in the way of this. So, let us go forth to make ourselves a joyous monkey. We'll use my son's drawing as our guide.

instructions

1. Let's start with a nice, deep-brown crew sock. You'll also need an accent color for Monkey's face, ears, paws, and tail tip. Check your Triple S for likely candidates, or rely on a trusty anklet. I'll use an aqua anklet now, for clarity. (That and because it mumbled something to me about today "being a good day to die." I don't know what it is with anklets…they're so dramatic.)

2. Cut the foot section off the brown sock, and snip off about 1½" (3.75 cm) of the toe section. Do not remove the stubby cuff from this sock. Cut the anklet into 3 pieces—1½" (3.75 cm) off the toe section, a 2" (5 cm) segment, and the remainder of the sock.

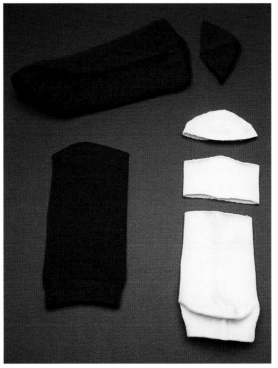

3. We'll sew Monkey's ears first. Cut the toe portion of both the brown and aqua socks so that you have 2 halves of each color. (You'll only need 1 of each.)

4. With right sides together, free-sew 2 little rounded monkey ears. Leave the bottoms open so you can turn them.

5. Trim away the excess, and turn the ears. Aren't they cute?

6. You could use what's left over from the foot section of the brown sock to complete this next step, but I'm going to cut up the other brown sock so you can see more clearly what I'm doing. Remove the stubby cuff, and cut off the foot section. This will leave you with a nice long piece in the middle to fashion Monkey's tail and arms. Remember that little 2″ (5 cm) aqua segment I had you cut earlier? We'll need that piece now, too.

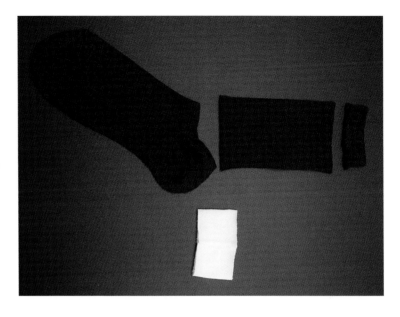

7. Slice open 1 side of the long brown segment and the aqua piece. Place them right sides together, and stitch across the top to attach them to each other.

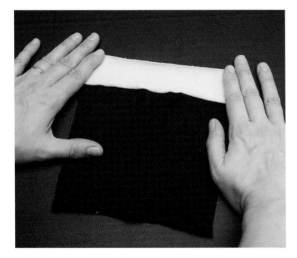

8. Fold this piece in half lengthwise. This is what you have to play with for sewing 2 arms and a tail. Free-sew 3 long, skinny tubes, each about the width of a pencil. Make the tail tube slightly skinnier, if you can.

9. Trim the seam allowances, and carefully turn each tube. Now you should have 2 lovely ears, 2 long arms, and 1 skinny tail.

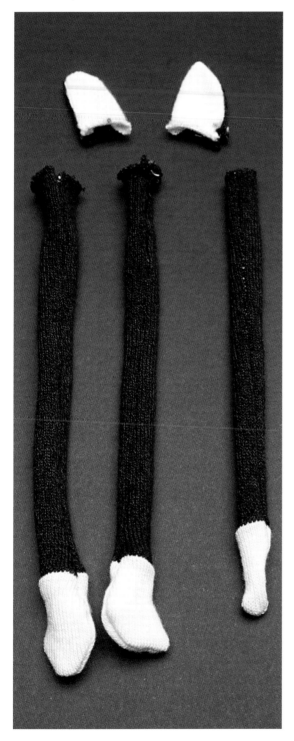

10. Remember the long brown cuffed piece from the first sock? Let's go back to that now. Turn this piece inside out. At the noncuff end, slide Monkey's ears between the top and bottom body pieces, with the rounded edges pointing inward. Pin in place.

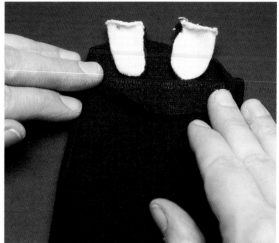

11. We'll lock these ears in place now by free-sewing just the top part of Monkey's head. She has a somewhat oval-shaped head. It's very wide, sewn almost to the edges of the sock, but not overly tall—about 1½″ (3.75 cm).

12. Carefully slice open the sides of Monkey's body tube. Now we'll insert her arms. Lay 1 arm between the front and back body as shown, and pin in place. Continue sewing where you left off on that side. Sew straight down, locking that first arm in place. Continue sewing to the bottom, and free-stitch 2 little short legs at the stubby cuff part of the sock.

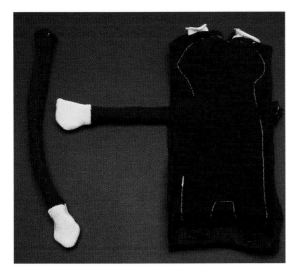

13. Tuck in the second arm (you might have to bunch it up in the center of the body to keep from sewing over the paw), and continue stitching.

14. Please remember to leave a small opening in Monkey's body, in order to turn her.

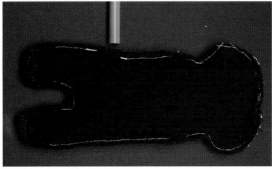

15. Already she is joyous. Just look at those hallelujah arms!

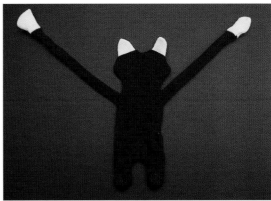

16. From the anklet, cut another segment slightly smaller than the width and depth of Monkey's head. Shape this piece into an oval. This will be her face.

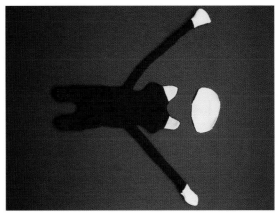

17. Before sewing on her face, gently stuff her with polyfill, and seal the opening in her body. Turn the raw edges of the face under. With a needle and matching thread, hand stitch the face onto the head.

18. Please give Monkey some eyes. You know my love for black seed beads…. Use 2 or 3 strands of black DMC floss to give her an enormous smile. I like to use a simple running stitch here, to give her a dotted smile. If you want her smile to be a continuous line, you can use a backstitch.

19. Not done yet! Monkey won't be truly joyous until she has a tail to swing from. You don't have to do this, but I like slipping a piece of pipe cleaner in the tail so that you can curl it around things. Just snip off any excess pipe cleaner, and slip stitch her tail to her butt.

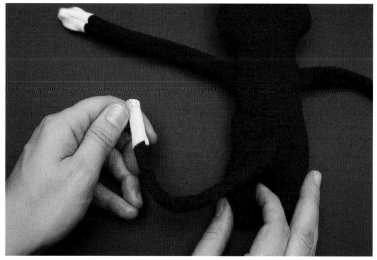

Doesn't she look joyous and ready to swing in the jungle now?

See no evil, hear no evil, speak no evil.

Monkey totem pole

Try adding an eye patch. Eye patches make anything more interesting.

Bananas for breakfast

Swinging in the jungle

Designed and made by Brenna Maloney.

raccoon

Finished size: About 8″ (20 cm) tall

A number of years ago, my family and I moved from the heart of Washington, D.C., to a house facing Rock Creek Park in an upper section of the city. Sounds lovely, doesn't it? Uh-huh. I thought so, too. On the first night in our new house, as I closed the drapes of the picture window in our living room, I saw a deer eating our mums. *Oh. Okay. Wildlife.* On the second night, I closed the drapes and saw a raccoon ambling across our front lawn. *Great.* On the third night, I saw a fox streaking across the yard. *Freakin' fan-tastic.* On the fourth night, I said to my husband, "*You* close the drapes!" True story. Anyway, it has been our ongoing relationships with the raccoons that have kept us the busiest. The little devils do so love our trash.

instructions

1. Find yourself a nice crew sock—angora, if you've got it. This will give some fluff to Raccoon's face. You'll just need the 1 sock. I'm going with a gray sock here, but you can try black, or, even better, find one with bands. Cut the foot segment off the sock.

2. From the foot segment near the toe, cut a triangle with slightly rounded sides from this piece, near the toe. You'll use this bit for the tail.

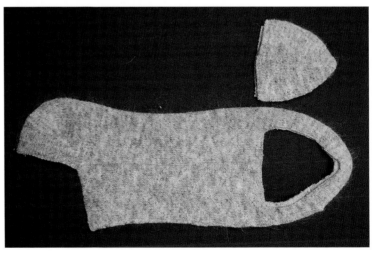

3. Cut away the little stripy part that's left over at the toe. Cut a 3″ (7.5 cm) tube from what's left, and set it aside.

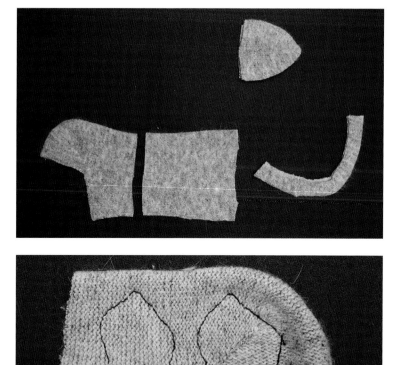

4. Turn the remaining heel section inside out, and free-sew a pair of ears, leaving them open at the bottom.

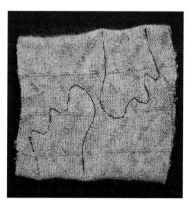

5. With right sides together, stitch up the tail, leaving it open at the base.

6. Turn the 3″ (7.5 cm) segment inside out, and free-sew 2 arms with 3-fingered hands. Set your machine to "Turtle," or whatever your slowest setting is, so that you can move like molasses in January while you sew these fingers. You'll thank me for this later. If you move too fast, you run the risk of giving Raccoon only 2 fingers. Or 4. Not that 3 is anatomically correct or anything. Okay, well, just be consistent, I guess. Or if not, have a good story to explain to your love ones how Two-Fingered Louie got his nickname.

7. Trim the seam allowances off these various and sundry parts I've had you sew, and turn them. You should have 2 ears, 2 arms (with an unconfirmed number of fingers), and a tail. Hmm…now all we need is a body.

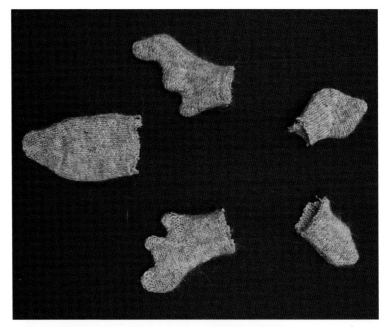

8. Oh, a body is easy enough. Use the upper part of the sock I had you cut off in Step 1. Turn it inside out. At the top, tuck the little ears in, upside down. You can pin them in place to keep them from going anywhere.

9. Now you are going to free-sew a raccoon body. Oh, yes. Just like that. Give Raccoon the most bulbous head you can manage. That may mean sewing clear out to the edges of the sock. And give him tiny, ridiculous-looking legs. Make sure as you sew that you leave a little opening somewhere to turn him.

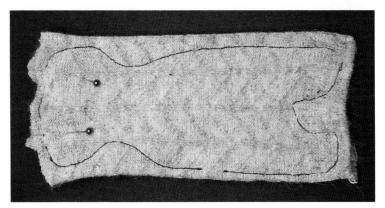

10. Trim away the excess, and turn him. His little ears should be nicely locked into place now. Let's go ahead and stuff him. Then sew up that opening you left for turning.

11. Stitch Raccoon's arms onto his sides by hand using a slip stitch. I centered each arm on the seam in his side. Be sure to turn the raw edges under and hide your stitches.

12. Attach his tail to his little bum. Turn the raw edges under, and hide your stitches, just as you did for his arms.

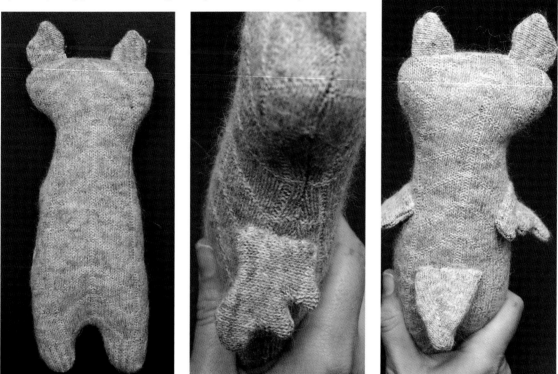

13. Set our little friend aside for a moment, and dig out some felt. We need to make him a proper mask so that when you catch him in your trash can, he'll look like the burglar he is. You'll need 2 small rectangles, 1 black and 1 white.

14. I've drawn up a mask pattern for you, in 2 sizes (page 61). The larger pattern is for the white felt; the smaller pattern is for the black felt. Cut both of these out.

15. Layer them, with white underneath. Place them across Raccoon's face, where his eyes should be. Using 2 to 3 strands of white DMC floss, stitch the masks in place, using a blanket stitch (see Stitch Gallery, page 14) and contrasting thread.

16. Inside the open ovals, give Raccoon tiny black seed beads for eyes. He's looking pretty good—although this fella is feeling remorse for having strewn trash all over your front yard. So we will use 2 to 3 strands of black DMC floss to give him an expression that matches his guilty conscience. (Although, in reality, they're never really that sorry.)

Raccoon Roundup

We've managed a pretty fine standard raccoon, but, like everything else in this book, there are many, many possible variations. Start with your sock choice—look for bands, colors, and patterns.

A chorus line...which way to your trash?

Conspiring to get your trash

"Who, us? Trash? Never heard of it."

And the masks. They look like thugs. I've given you a standard pattern, but you can play with both color and shape.

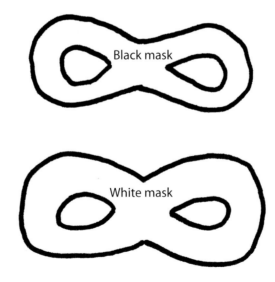

Black mask

White mask

Designed and made by Brenna Maloney.

sheep

Finished size: About 5″ (12.75 cm) tall

You'll need to display some sheeplike tendencies for this pattern! You'll need to follow my precise directions with great care. (Stop snickering. I can be precise when I want to. Well, pretty much.) We're gonna mix things up a bit. We're gonna get a little crazy here. Head into your kitchen, and bring back a cooling rack. You know what I'm talking about? One of those wire deals that you cool cookies on? Yes, it's okay to eat some of the cookies first.

instructions

1. Find a pair of long knee-highs—thigh-highs, if you've got them. You'll also need some scraps or an anklet. Think "sheep." You *can* go with straight white or gray, but you might also want to consider a nice polka dot. Here I've chosen gray with pink polka dots and another pink sock for my scrap. You'll also need a piece of muslin—roughly 3" × 5" (7.5 cm × 12.75 cm), depending on what size your sheep's body turns out to be in Step 9.

2. You're also gonna need some Pellon Wonder Under. Have you ever heard of this stuff? It's a paper-backed fusible web that you iron onto fabric. It gives the fabric extra strength. It's pretty cool stuff, and we are going to use it when we sew our sheep!

3. Let's get started with 1 of the knee-highs. I'll show you what to do with this first sock. There will be a quiz and a speed test on the second sock. You will have to perform the same steps blindfolded, using only a rusty axe for cutting. Keeps things interesting. For right now, cut off the toe section, and discard the cuff.

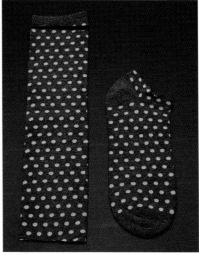

4. Slice open the sock tube on 1 side to make a nice, long rectangle.

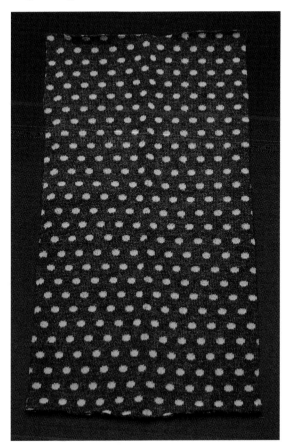

5. Place the sock facedown on the cooling rack, and go find an unsharpened pencil.

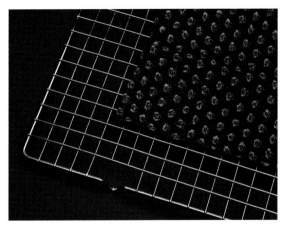

6. What you're going to do now might seem pretty weird, but just go with it, okay? With the pencil, poke the sock through the little squares on the cooling rack—just enough to create a bubble effect on the other side. If your rack just has lines in one direction and not a grid, stack two racks together with the bars perpendicular to each other. Start in the middle of the sock, and work your way outward. As you do this, the sock is going to shrink up because you are pushing so much of it through to the other side. You should still end up with a rectangle, just a much smaller one than the one you started with.

7. Flip the rack over and make sure the bubbles look relatively even and that, in your zeal, you haven't poked any holes through. Perfection is absolutely not required here.

8. Now cut a piece of Pellon the exact size of your shriveled-up bubbled sock. I know, it's looking really unsightly now, but trust me. Place the Pellon *sticky side down* over the back of the sock (the side you were poking, not the bubbled side).

9. Carry the entire cooling rack to your ironing area. Set your iron on the wool setting and place a paper towel over the Pellon and sock. Press firmly for 10 to 15 seconds, and then let the sock cool for a few minutes. Remove the paper towel and gently peel back the paper. Your ugly, shriveled sock should look much worse now because it is coated in a filmy, sticky white coating. This is good!

10. Now cut a piece of muslin a little larger than your sticky, bubbled sock, and iron the muslin on top of the sticky side. Let that cool for a few minutes.

11. *Very* gently, peel the entire mess off the cooling rack. What should happen is that the bubbles remain, and the sock now has a firm muslin backing.

12. Repeat Steps 3 through 11 with the other knee-high. But set your stopwatch—this is the speed test part of this exercise! These panels will be your sheep's body.

13. Now we're going to make 4 legs and a tail. Compared to what you just went through, this next part ain't so bad! Cut a 3" (7.5 cm) segment of polka dot sock from the foot section and a 1" (2.5 cm) segment of pink sock. These will make 2 legs and a tail; you'll need to repeat with the other socks to make 2 more legs.

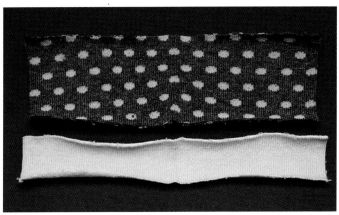

14. Slice both tubes open on 1 side, and lay them flat. The polka dot part will be the leg; the pink part will be the hoof. Stitch the strips together.

15. Fold the strip in half, and free-sew several long rectangles. You can probably eke out 2 legs and a tail. The tail should look the same as the legs, only skinnier. Repeat Steps 13 through 15 to make the other 2 legs.

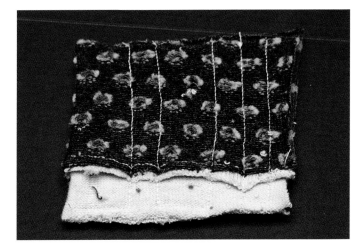

16. Find a pink scrap, and free-sew 2 ears.

17. Trim the seam allowances off the legs and ears, and carefully turn everything.

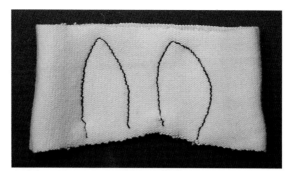

18. From a 3″ (7.5 cm) section of pink sock, free-cut a sheep's head. This isn't too difficult. You know what a sheep looks like, right? In case you are uncertain, I've included a small guide showing you what is and is not a sheep's head. This isn't really a pattern, exactly, just a guide, because the head should be proportional to the body. I'm not exactly sure how big your bubbled-up rectangles are, but I trust you completely to eyeball it.

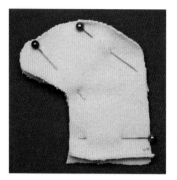

This is a sheep. Pick this one!

NOT a sheep.

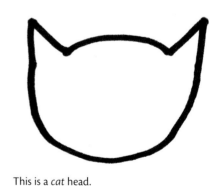

This is a *cat* head.

19. Use a rotary cutter to slice a very small slit at a slight angle on each side piece of Sheep's head. Note that no fingers were lost in the making of this sheep's head. Of course, it always helps if you start out with 11 fingers, with 1 for a spare. Slip the ears through the slits, and stitch them in place on the wrong side.

20. With right sides together and ears inside, stitch together the 2 head pieces, leaving the neck open. Turn it right side out.

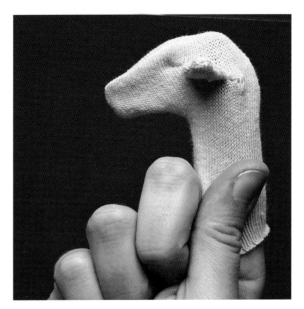

21. Return to your bubbled rectangles, and place them bubble sides together, with the muslin facing out. Free-sew an oval for the body. Think about your sheep as you go. How would you like her to look? Is she plump? Is she long and skinny? Be sure to leave a fairly wide neck hole. And you might want to backstitch on both ends, just to give the seam extra strength when turning. Trim off the excess.

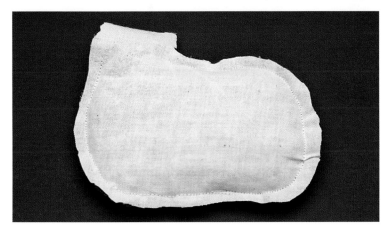

22. *Very* gently turn Sheep's body. If you're too rough, you could unbubble the bubbles. I'm really proud of you. This is a long and tough pattern, and you're holding up beautifully. Now we're going to start putting all the pieces together. Stuff the head and body with polyfill.

23. Insert the neck into the opening on the body. Turn under the edges on the body to create a smooth line. Using a needle and matching thread, slip stitch the head to the body. Nicely done!

24. Now for Sheep's legs. To make them strong, use a bit of bent pipe cleaner. Just make a U shape and cut off the excess. Do this for all 4 legs (but not the tail). Insert a U into each leg, and pack polyfill around it. Sew on the legs and tail. She's looking great and standing on her own 4 legs now!

25. Let's add some eyes. Yeah, I know—more black seed beads! What's my deal with those? I dunno. You can use something else if you like; it won't bother me.

26. Two or 3 strands of black DMC will complete Sheep's face. I've given her an upside-down Y, but I'll admit she looks a little sad. You might want to make her more cheerful.

That was a lot of hard work, but she looks great!

Stitch a Flock

There are ways to vary this pattern. If you'd like Sheep to be resting in the field instead of grazing, don't sew any legs. If you want to make a little lamb baby for her, just make everything a bit smaller. Or make some Hampshire sheep with black faces.

Designed and made by Brenna Maloney.

zebra

Finished size: About 20″ (51 cm) tall

Whenever I see black and white stripes, I think prison. Although, technically, I think prisoners mostly wear orange these days. I wouldn't last five minutes in prison, and that's the truth. Which is why, when I briefly considered bank robbery as a career choice, I decided against it. Think of the jumpsuit, I told myself. Who looks good in orange? And they always give you one that's too baggy. How are you supposed to look tough in a baggy orange jumpsuit?

Better to stay law abiding. Better to keep myself off the mean streets at night by sewing little animals out of socks. Like, you know, a striped zebra.

instructions

1. You'll need 1 very long striped thigh-high (or 2 long knee-highs). I cheated a little and used a pair of stripy black-and-white tights. They sell these around Halloween sometimes. For grown women to wear. Do they actually wear them? I think if you were going to, you'd have to accessorize with a pointed hat and a broomstick, maybe. Not me. No. I just buy them to cut into little pieces.

2. If you managed to procure a pair of grown-lady witchy-tights, you'll need only 1 leg. Cut that leg off at the hip. The height of the zebra is going to depend on the length of this leg. Cut it in 3 pieces, as shown. You'll use the longest segment for Zebra's body, the shorter segment for his arms, and the foot section for his head.

3. Let's start with his head. If you've slogged through the Sheep pattern (page 62), I know I can just tell you to cut out a zebra head and you'll know what I'm talking about. If not, just remember that zebras have heads roughly shaped like horses' heads, but with shorter noses. If you're working with stripes, inch yourself down to the toe tip where, in my case here, there is a black band. I wanted Zebra's nose to be black, so I cut around this area to form his head.

4. Go into your sewing lair, and rifle through your things until you find something interesting like fringe, yarn, or ribbon that you can use as a mane. If you're working with ribbon, as I am here, cut off little segments that you can loop.

5. Pin these little loops around 1 side of Zebra's head, pointing inward as shown.

6. Place the other side of his head on top, right sides together, to sandwich in the mane, and stitch along the top of the nose and back of the neck. Turn the head, and have a look.

7. Using a leftover black piece from the toe section, free-sew yourself 2 little Zebra ears, trim, and turn them.

8. With your trusty rotary cutter, make ear slits in Zebra's head on both sides. We'll need these to be able to insert and sew his ears.

9. Turn the head inside out again. Insert the ears so they face toward the nose, and carefully, slowly stitch them in place on the wrong side.

10. Now stitch the rest of Zebra's head, leaving the neck open, of course. Turn it to have a look.

11. Take the shorter piece we cut in Step 2, turn it inside out, and free-sew 2 long, skinny "arms" just a little more than a pencil's width. At the bottom, give Zebra rounded black hooves.

12. Cut away the excess, and gently turn. If you use an unsharpened pencil, it should go easily enough. Take your time.

13. Now take that last, long piece from Step 2, and turn it inside out. Fold an end in half. Cut in from the sides to make a tapered neck. Just shape it a little so that when you open it up, Zebra's shoulders are sloped.

14. Slice open the sides of the body. To be honest, I don't usually slice all the way down—just enough to work the arms in.

15. Tuck 1 of the turned arms in on the open side. Pin in place, and begin sewing that side.

16. Here, you can decide how tall you want your zebra to be; mine is the whole sock length. When you get to the bottom of this first side, sew 2 skinny little legs. I made mine fairly thin, and, to make them even, I counted out 7 stripes on each leg.

17. We still have that second arm to get in, so sandwich and pin it in on the other open side. To get the arms out of the way, I just dragged them up through the neck hole while I sewed.

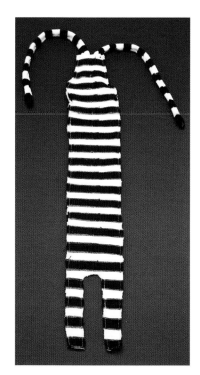

18. Turn Zebra right side out, and begin stuffing with polyfill, starting with his legs. Take your time, and pack the polyfill tightly. Gradually work your way up until you've stuffed the entire body. Go ahead and also stuff the head.

19. It's time to attach the head to the body. I inserted the head inside the neck, turned under the neck's raw edges, and hand stitched the head in place using matching thread and a slip stitch (page 14).

20. A black seed bead works nicely for an eye.

Slice of Zebra Life

Nonconformist zebras

Designed and made by Brenna Maloney.

kangaroo and joey

Finished size: About 8″ (20 cm) tall

Plenty of absurd things in Nature. Take the kangaroo. Picture life as a baby kangaroo. It's *dark* in that pouch. Gotta be, right? Maybe a little claustrophobic, too? And there's all that bouncing around. I mean, it's different when you are the one in control of the bouncing. Then it might be fun. But when Mom's driving, hippity hopping all over the place—UP and down and UP and down—and you're squeezed up in that suffocating little pouch, well, it's enough to make *me* puke just thinking about it. So if baby kangaroos ever make it to adulthood, you know they are tough little buggers. We'll make one of out of a sock. It will be sweet looking. Only you will know it how tough its hide really is.

One note: Be sure to have on hand some Junior Mints or other candy of your choice. Something to help calm your nerves while you attempt to sew itty-bitty sock pieces together. I'll be honest—this pattern requires nerves of steel.

instructions

1. For a kangaroo and baby, you'll need 1 long fuzzy angora knee-high. Probably a light color—white, tan, or a pastel.

2. We're going to cut this sock *very* carefully. There will be a billion little pieces. Okay, I might be slightly overstating things. But there *are* a whole big bunch. Start by cutting the sock into 3 large chunks, as pictured. The middle section will be Kangaroo's body; the foot and the sock top sections will make up her different parts.

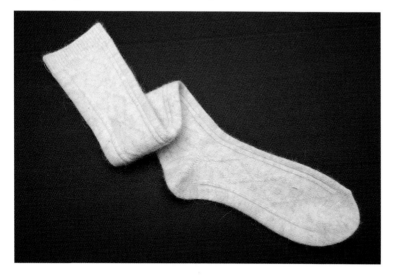

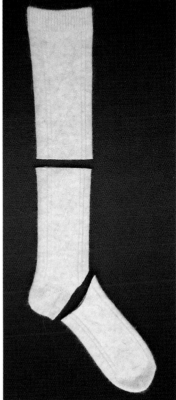

3. Cut the tip of the toe off the rest of its piece at about 2½" (6.25 cm).

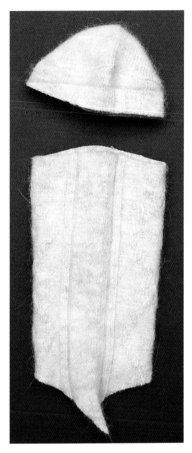

4. Turn that toe piece inside out; cut, and then sew it, in 3 pieces. The middle piece is a long rectangle, sewn on 3 sides. This is Kangaroo's pouch. The 2 triangles on each end will be Kangaroo's paws.

5. Turn the remaining foot section inside out, and free-sew 2 leg-and-foot shapes as shown. Leave a tiny opening in each haunch so you can turn it. Remember, kangaroos do a lot of hopping, so their haunches are large and their feet are long and thin.

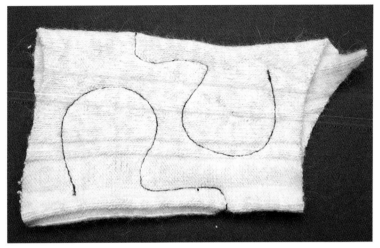

6. From the sock top section, we are now going to cut 3 odd-shaped pieces. Why? Because this pattern simply wasn't miserable enough yet. We need a tail for Kangaroo, so cut that from the top. Make it long and tapered at the end. The middle swatch will be mostly scrap, although we can use it for ears. The small rectangle we will use for Kangaroo's baby.

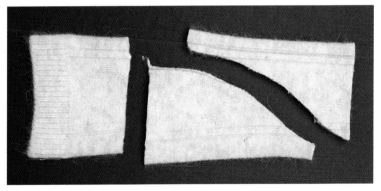

7. Free-sew a small pair of ears out of *your* scrap. Notice I say *your* scrap. At this point, I know you are starting to mutter swear words under your breath. This is a good time for me to start to back away slowly… and pretend I don't know you.

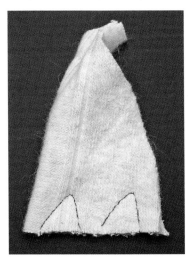

8. Free-sew the shape of a little joey from the rectangular piece. The baby doesn't need much detail—just go for the general shape. Be sure to leave a small opening so you can turn her.

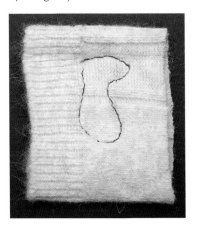

9. Stitch up Kangaroo's tail; trim, and then gently turn, all these little pieces.

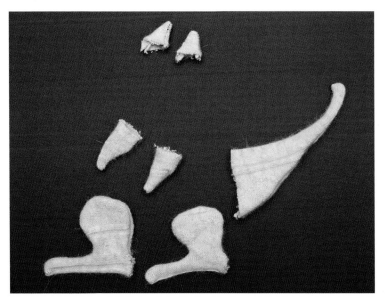

10. Go back to the middle sock section that I told you we'd be using for Kangaroo's body. Lay this piece flat. You'll make a small incision—not much more than ½″ (1.25 cm) wide—in her tummy, so we can insert her pouch. Use small scissors and *cut only the front layer of the sock.* Try not to cut any fingers. I'm not sure the best way to get blood out of angora, and I'd hate for you to bleed to death while I try to look it up on the Internet.

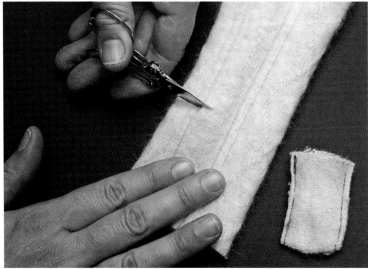

11. Insert the pouch, and sew along the top front pocket edge. You might want to sew it in place by hand. It should form a nice little pocket.

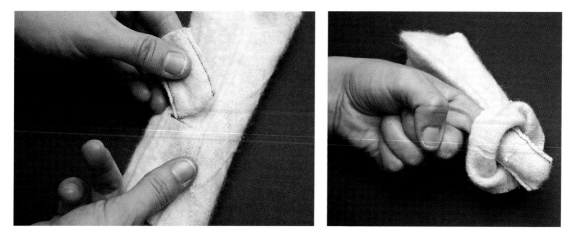

12. For the little pointed paws, snip off a segment of pipe cleaner, and bend to form a V. Insert 1 into each paw.

13. Make 2 very small incisions into Kangaroo's chest so we can insert her paws. You might feel like a surgeon on a prime-time doctor show when you do this. Just move slowly and steadily. You can rest during the commercial break. With the paws in position, hand stitch, hand stitch, hand stitch them into place.

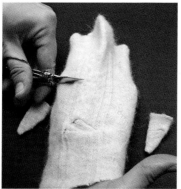

14. Turn Kangaroo inside out again. We need to stitch the poor dear's head. Start at the top of her nose and follow the line down, finishing up with her back.

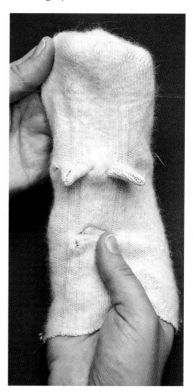

15. Now stuff Kangaroo. Then, using a running stitch all around the sock bottom, cinch it together. Knot it firmly.

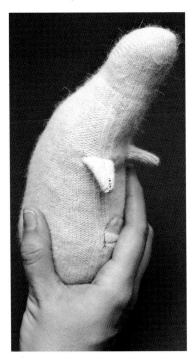

16. We'll add the tail next. Stuff it firmly, and hand sew it on.

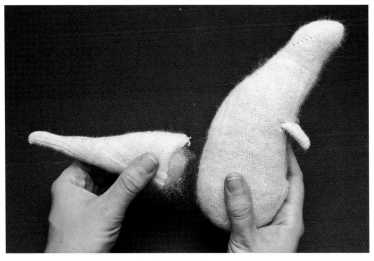

17. Gently stuff Kangaroo's legs, and stitch closed the small opening you used to turn them. Hand stitch them to her body.

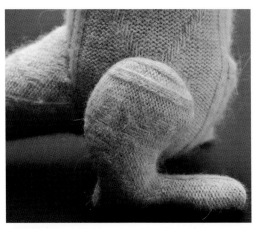

18. Hand stitch her tiny, tiny ears to her head. Oh, man. If you're still speaking to me after you get those ears on, then I *know* we're friends. And add eyes. Black seed beads, anyone?

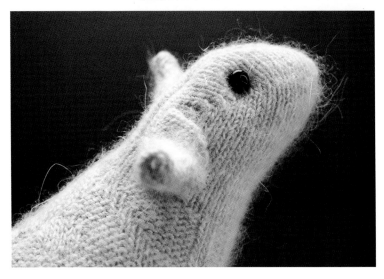

19. It's time to get Joey ready! She needs the tinniest amount of stuffing. But be sure to pad her butt. With all that bouncing she's going to endure, she'll need the extra padding. Seal her opening. Give her eyes. She's very small!

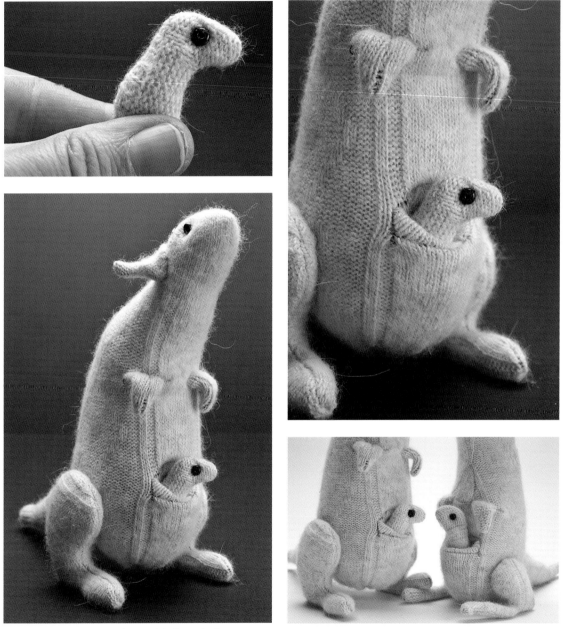

And here's Mama K, complete with baby tucked into her pouch.

Never too young to network!

Here comes Helga. Check out those thunder thighs! That's what you get when you use too thick of a sock!

And this one? Don't be fooled. That's no lady. It's a male kangaroo. You can tell by his profile. That's not a real pouch...it's his "murse," or man-purse to carry the baby. His wife works. He's a liberated 'roo, in touch with his feminine side.

Designed and made by Brenna Maloney.

bear

Finished size: About 9″ (23 cm) tall

All I can hear in my head right now, besides the usual voices, is Ballou, the bear from the Disney kids' movie, "The Jungle Book." He's singing, "Look for the bare necessities, the simple bare necessities, forget about your worry and your strife…." Ah, if only. Well, maybe for a little while, eh? Let's ditch the worry and strife and have some fun making Bear. You'll like this one. His sense of rhythm isn't quite as good as Ballou's, but his arms and legs can actually move.

instructions

1. To make Bear, look for a pair of knee-highs, any color.

2. This is a pattern with a whole lotta pieces to it. Sorry about that. Laying it out can be a bit of a nightmare, so take a look at this photo for some guidance. You can cut most of the pieces from the first sock.

3. Cut the remaining arm, leg, and ear from the second sock.

4. Separate the front and back pieces of Bear's torso, and fold each in half, right sides together. Sew little darts where the pattern indicates.

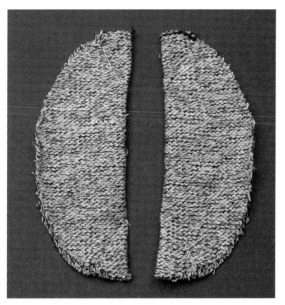

5. Sew the front and back pieces together, leaving a small opening for turning.

6. Turn Bear's body now. He's going to have a round little tum.

7. With right sides together, stitch his ears together, keeping the bottoms open. Also stitch his arms together, leaving a small gap to turn them.

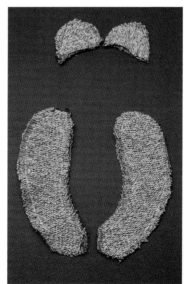

8. Let's get the legs under way. Stitch the leg pieces together, leaving the bottoms open for foot pads.

9. The foot pads will help the bear stand up. When you sew them in place, leave a tiny opening for turning. Look! Not even turned yet, but already standing.

10. Now we'll work on Bear's head. This pattern has a gusset. When you sew it in place, you'll also sew on the ears. Place the head gusset and 1 head side piece right sides together, matching up the X's, and sandwich an ear, point facing inward, in between. Start at the nose, and sew all the way to the back of the neck. You can turn Bear to make sure the ear is locked in place.

11. Flip the head right side out again, sew the second side and ear, and turn.

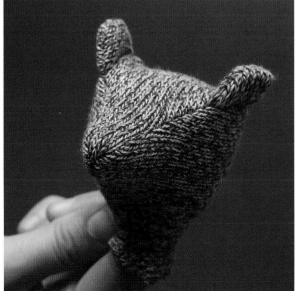

12. Stuff Bear's tummy and seal up the opening. Stuff his head as well. Turn the raw edges of his neck under, and slip stitch the head to the body.

13. And now the fun begins. (Full disclosure: This is sarcasm. I do not really mean that the next few steps will be fun. In fact, they may border on miserable. Sorry about this. Some suffering on your part will be required in order to give Bear really cool arms and legs that move. Suck it up. You can do this.) Look in your lair for 4 buttons and some heavy-duty thread. I use carpenter's thread, which can be found in a sewing store like Jo-Ann Fabrics. You'll also need the longest needle you can find. If you have one that is 6" (15 cm) long, you're golden. If you have one that long, can you tell me where you got it? Because mine is only about 2" (5 cm) inches long.

14. We're going to attach Bear's limbs 2 at a time in such a way that they can move. He's got hunting to do, this one. He's got fish to catch and roots to unearth. He needs his mobility. Let's start with his legs.

15. Make a Dagwood sandwich: button, leg, bear, leg, button. Poke the needle in through the first button, and pull it all the way through Bear's body and out through the second button. This might be a little awkward. If you're struggling, you might want to try a pair of pliers. I used my teeth, but my publisher said that I should not tell you that, nor should I advise you under any circumstances to use your teeth. So, you know,

don't do that. Get the pliers. Pass the needle through several times until the limbs feel secure. Don't cinch too tight, now. You're not trying to squeeze Miss Scarlett into her corset. If you've done everything correctly, you should have movement! Repeat with the arms.

16. Add some button eyes, and satin stitch a small nose on Bear (see Stitch Gallery, page 14), and he's ready to hit the forest!

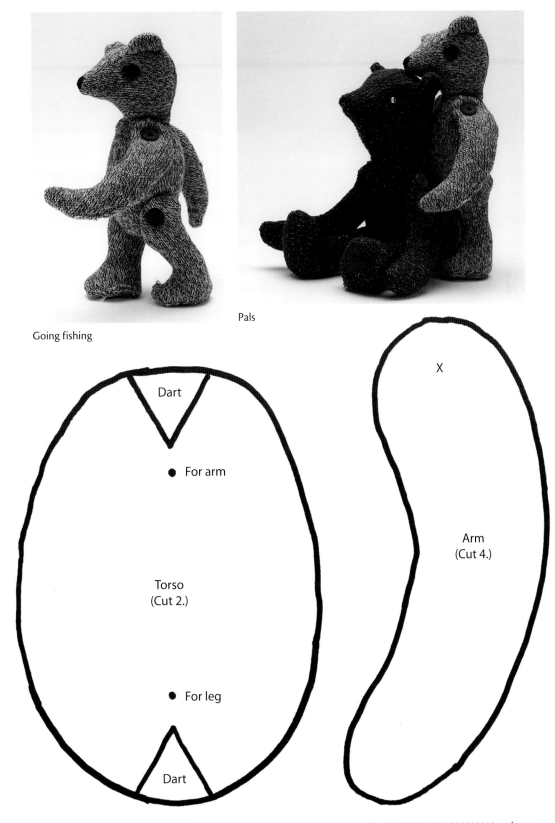

Going fishing

Pals

Dart

For arm

Torso
(Cut 2.)

For leg

Dart

X

Arm
(Cut 4.)

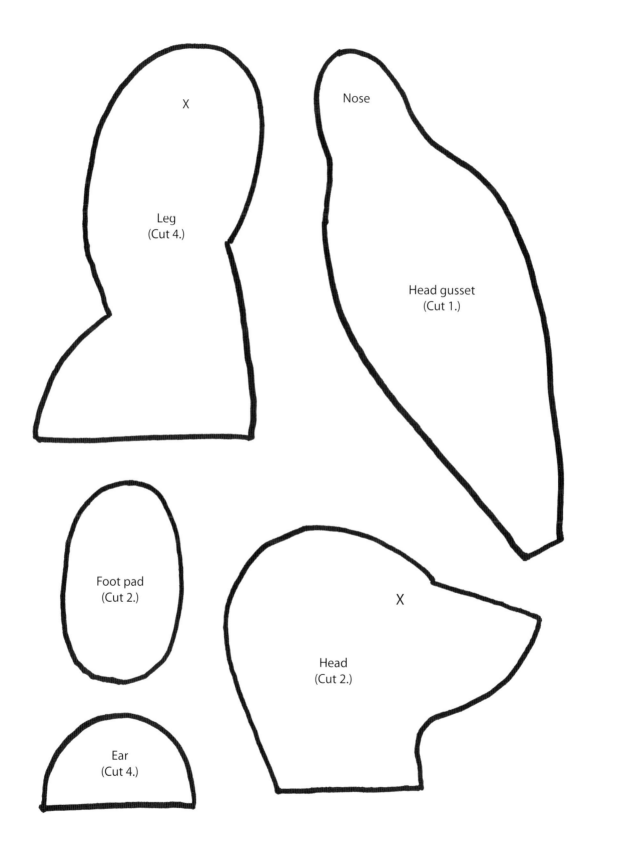

Leg
(Cut 4.)

X

Nose

Head gusset
(Cut 1.)

Foot pad
(Cut 2.)

X

Head
(Cut 2.)

Ear
(Cut 4.)

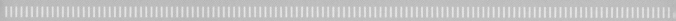

things that swim...

Designed and made by Brenna Maloney.

shark

Finished size: About 17″ (43 cm) long

The Hammerhead shark, well, she's a badass, isn't she? With a head like that? She'd have to be. She's out there, cruising the ocean waters looking for a snack, just like any other thousand-pound beast with serrated teeth. Except that she's gotta be extra tough because the Great Whites are always thundering by, calling her "Popeye" and saying disparaging things about her parentage. Okay, so she's not as big as the Great White. And she's got eye "issues." So what? She's got game. Her funky eyes make her a better hunter. And she can scarf down manta rays with the best of them.

instructions

1. For this beastie, you'll need 1½ socks, which is sort of awkward. But just stash that extra half in your Triple S (page 9) for later. I used matching knee-highs. Mine have these strange little pom-poms on them. I cannot explain that. I just cut them off. Madam Hammerhead has no need for such frivolity. She's a natural killer, you know.

2. Cut the first sock as follows. Get rid of the cuff (and any offending pom-poms that may or may not be connected), and cut off the toe section. This leaves a long tube—the longer, the better.

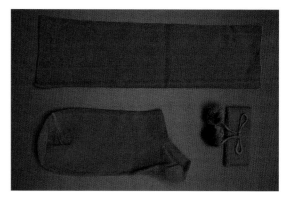

3. We'll start with the head. You can free-sew a hammer-shaped head if you like. If free-sewing seems too scary—and it was for me—I've provided another bit of bad art for us to use as a pattern (see page 99). Turn the foot of the sock inside out, and use the pattern to mark the hammer shape. Then cut it out.

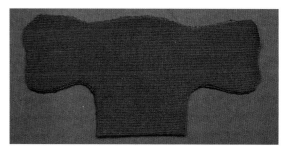

4. From the second half sock, mark and cut 2 pectoral fins and 1 dorsal fin, all double-layered, also using the patterns (page 99).

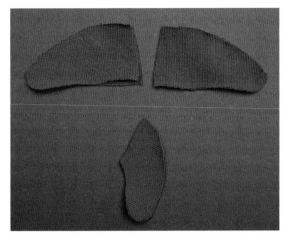

5. With right sides together, sew together the pieces for the head and all 3 fins.

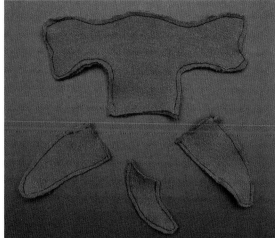

6. Now go back to the long tube. Do forgive me, but this *is* one of those cases where I am going to suggest that you cut away everything that doesn't look like a shark body. At the end, cut a tail. I've made some pretty lousy tails in my time, but essentially, you're going to cut a tail with 2 "lobes"—an upper lobe and a smaller, lower lobe. Now don't be hard on yourself, here. Remember, if *I* can do it, *anybody* can do it.

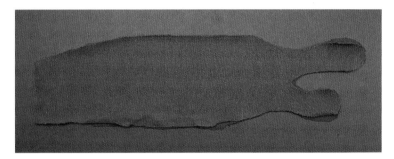

7. Before you sew Shark's body, you'll need to insert her dorsal fin and hand stitch it in place. The fin needs to point backward. Do concentrate while you're doing this. If you are distracted, there is a very great chance that you will sew it facing the wrong direction. I'm not sure, but that might cause her to perpetually swim backward, not to mention the fact that it would *really tick her off!*

8. Sew up Shark's body, leaving the neck open, and you're ready to attach her head. With right sides together, match the raw edges of the head and body openings, and pin the head in place. Hand sew slowly around the neck, leaving a small opening to turn her.

9. Go ahead and turn Madam Hammerhead. She's looking lifeless, but she will feel better after she eats some polyfill.

10. Take your time, and really pack the polyfill tightly. I started with her back end and worked my way up, stuffing the head last. Make sure you really push the polyfill into her eye sockets. You may need to work the head with your hands to give it a well-defined shape.

11. With a needle and matching thread, slipstitch Shark's neck opening closed. And while you're at it, hand stitch her 2 pectoral fins underneath her body.

12. She's looking good, but she needs some eyes. Shank buttons work well because they tend to stick out a bit on the sides of the head. Once her eyes are in place, she's ready to go hunting for prey!

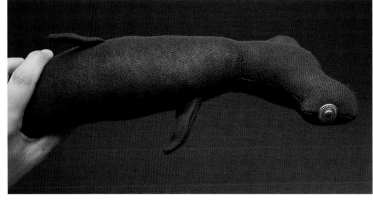

"Where's the prey, Mom? Huh? Huh? I'm starving!"

Sneaky shark on tiptoe

Gang on the prowl

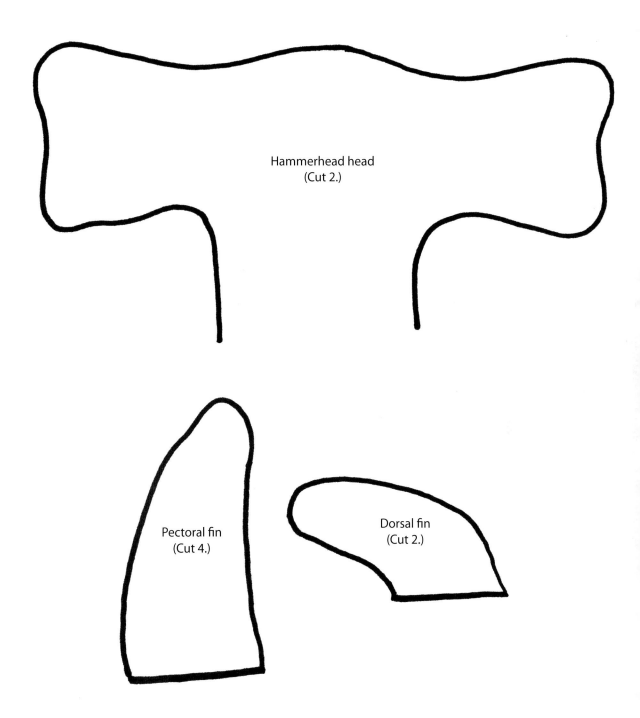

Hammerhead head
(Cut 2.)

Pectoral fin
(Cut 4.)

Dorsal fin
(Cut 2.)

Designed and made by Brenna Maloney.

crocodile

Finished size: About 25″ (63.5 cm) long

Crocs. They get such a bad rap. Okay, so they've got razor-sharp teeth. And they do that vicious death roll thing with their prey underwater. But, hey, they've got a softer side, too. I'm sure. Well, maybe not mine. Mine just seem to want to eat things. You'll see.

instructions

1. Crocodile requires long, long, really long socks: knee-highs, thigh-highs, tights—whatever. You'll need the pair, and you'll need an anklet in a contrasting color for the inside of Croc's mouth.

2. Cut the foot section off the first sock, rounding an end. Open it—see? You have Croc's mouth.

3. Turn the anklet inside out. Insert it toe first into the mouth you just created.

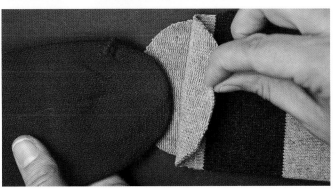

4. Trim the anklet right at Croc's lips. Do crocodiles have lips? I don't really know. Well, whatever. You know what I'm referring to.

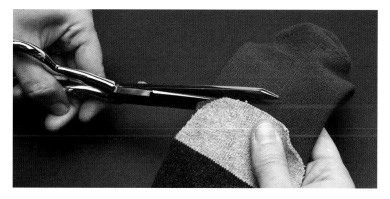

5. Slice down the sides of Croc's mouth a bit to widen the opening.

6. Now. You'll need a zipper. A 9″ (23 cm) ought to do nicely. It can be the same color as the sock or a contrasting color.

note

Oh, I thought it would be so cool and so clever to have Croc's mouth open and close with a zipper. Yeah, well, when I first attempted this, I realized that I couldn't remember how to sew in a zipper! Oh, so embarrassing. But, honestly, what do *I* sew that requires a zipper? The last zipper I successfully installed was in eighth-grade home ec class, for Pete's sake. Well, the whole thing became a little paralyzing. I sized up the zipper against the mouth. And then, well, I hate to admit it, but...I just guessed. Disclaimer: Author is no longer responsible for her actions or for the success of this project. If you yourself know how to install a zipper, do so now and then skip ahead to Step 11. If you, like the author, can't remember how to install a zipper, either ask your mother to do it or stick with the author. Your call.

7. Here's how I did it. Turning under the raw edges of the "lips," I nervously pinned the top part of Croc's mouth to 1 side of the blasted zipper.

8. Next, I flipped the zipper over Croc, and, turning under the raw edges of the red mouth lining, I pinned that part to the flip side of the zipper, so half the zipper was sandwiched in between the inner and outer "lips."

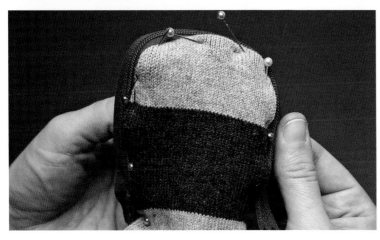

9. I opened the zipper. Then, I stitched close to the zipper teeth through all the layers to finish half of the mouth. (Mrs. Dunn, my eighth-grade home ec teacher—wherever she is—must have had a seizure at that moment. Deep in her bones, she would have felt, "One of my students is screwing up a simple zipper.")

10. Well, when the zipper police (or Mrs. Dunn) failed to show up at my doorstep to arrest or fine me, I went ahead and pinned the lower jaw, just as I did the upper jaw, and stitched that side of the zipper.

11. Then I closed the zipper and wept with relief.

12. Onward! Take that foot section you lopped off in Step 2 and turn it inside out. Free-sew 4 feet. Now, crocodile feet, I believe, are sort of wide things with 5 toes. I chose not to be anatomically correct and gave Croc only 3. Whatever you think works.

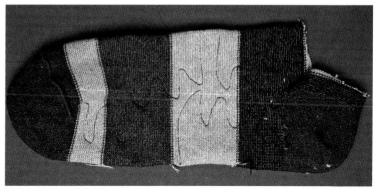

13. Trim off the excess, and turn. You should have 4 far-from-perfect-looking Croc feet.

14. From the second long sock, cut off a long section and free-sew about 10 pointies of different heights and widths for the ridges on Croc's back. If you're working with a striped sock, try sewing the pointies on the edges of color bands so that each pointy is 2 colors.

15. Trim the seam allowances, and turn for a nice pile of ridges.

16. The next few steps might make you squeamish because it will look like I'm wrecking everything. But if you stuck by me through that zipper fiasco, I know you will trust me now. Lay Croc flat, and cut a long line down the middle of his back—from the end of the sock to right before you reach the head/zippered part. (Cut only the top layer!)

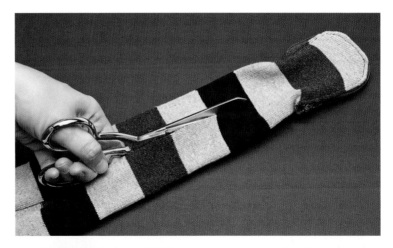

17. Try not to flinch as you to slice open both sides as well.

18. Good grief. What have we done?

19. It's okay. Really. Take the 2 pieces that were once Croc's back, and, with right sides together, start slipping the pointies in along 1 edge, facing inward. Space them evenly along the spine, and pin through the pointies and both body layers so they don't shift around when you sew.

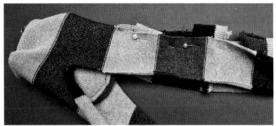

20. Sew along Croc's back, stitching the pointies in place. Flip Croc over to get a look at him so far. Very nice.

21. Make sure the Croc's body is inside out. On the sides we split, lay in his feet, 2 on each side. You can space them evenly or angle them so he looks like he is walking with one leg in front of the other. Remember to place the feet toe side in first.

22. Stitch along Croc's body on both sides with the front sides together, trapping the feet and leaving a small opening on 1 side to turn him. Trim off any excess seam allowance.

23. Give Croc a turn. He looks a bit odd here, I know, but we're getting there.

24. Stuff, stuff, stuff him. Start with the tail, and work your way up to the head. Stuff him firmly. Use a slip stitch to close the opening.

25. Find Croc a nice pair of large eyes. Something colorful, to match the inside of his mouth, perhaps?

With his eyes in place, he's ready for his next death roll in the mud with a struggling wildebeest. Good times!

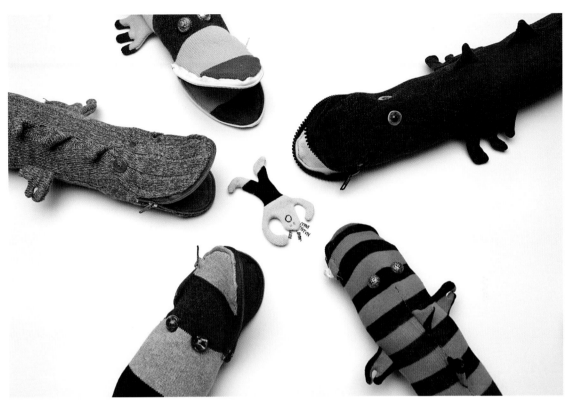

"I saw him first." "No, I saw him first!" "You got the last one…"

"Mine, all mine…"

Designed and made by Brenna Maloney.

frog

Finished size: About 17″ (43 cm) tall

I'm sure you know that frogs have teeth (and toads do not). Don't ask me how I know that. It's stored in the same part of my brain that can sing the periodic table and recite the Victor Hugo poem "Autumn" in French, and ask you, "Where is the nearest bathroom?" in Canadian. But the coolest thing about frogs, of course, is their ability to hop like little fiends. In the sock version of Frog, we want to pay homage to this remarkable ability, so for this pattern, it's all about the feet.

instructions

1. Oh! Striped! Striped socks are so fun for Frog. You'll need a knee-high with really strong colors. You'll also need to scrounge up a colorful anklet.

2. Start by cutting the striped sock a few stripes from the heel toward the toe. Cut the anklet into 4 pieces, 2 of which should be 1½" (3.75 cm)-wide segments. Cut open the 1½" (3.75 cm)-wide segments along 1 side.

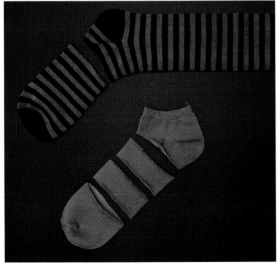

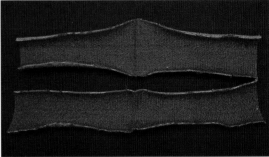

3. Open the 1½″ (3.75 cm)-wide segments flat and stitch the ends together to make 1 long strip. What am I doing, you ask? Shh…it's a secret. Ha! No. I'm only kidding. It is not a secret. You are making frog lips. Yes, of course frogs have lips.

4. Fold under an end of the strip, and fold the whole strip in half lengthwise. Now pass "Go" and collect your $200.

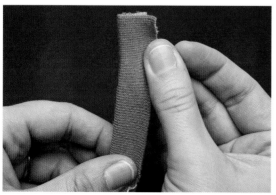

5. Turn the long section of the striped sock inside out, and pin the pink strip along the edges of the opening, on the heel end. Take your time, and pin the strip in place all the way around the opening.

6. Sew the strip in place.

8. Turn the piece right side out to examine the beautiful frog lips. No Botox needed! See? I told you anklets were useful. You'll see when you stuff Frog how expressive those lips can make his face. You can turn them down or put a corner up just by adjusting them with your fingers.

7. Fold the opening over so that the strip is on the inside. Stitch across the opening through all the layers.

9. Take what's left of the toe section of the striped sock, turn it inside out, and free-sew 2 long frog arms with 2 fingers. Why 2 fingers? No reason—none at all. It's not like I said to myself, "The more fingers I sew, the more I have to turn. Oh, look! Two is good!" No, no, it was nothing like that at all.

10. Carefully trim away the excess, and turn Frog's arms. Don't rush. See suggestions for turning without losing your mind (page 13).

11. Make sure Frog's body is inside out. Slice open part of his sides, up where his shoulders might be.

12. Insert his arms, with his fingers pointing inward.

13. Sew his shoulders together on each side, trapping each arm.

14. Now let's sew the rest of Frog's body. From where you stopped with his arms, continue to sew down toward the end of the sock. Set your machine on "Turtle," and advance as slowly as possible as you free-sew 2 long-toed frog feet.

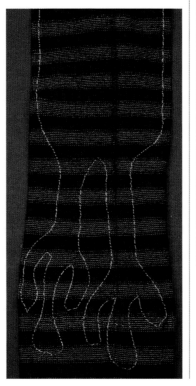

note

Let's discuss those toes. Just as I don't care how many fingers you give him, I also don't care how many toes you give him. But toes of some number you must give him because he is a hip-hoppity frog. I recommend three. I tend to make frog toes exceptionally long—sometimes nearly two inches. It depends on how much sock you have, really. If I sew three toes on each foot, I usually make the middle toe the longest.

15. I hope you remembered to leave a small gap for turning. This is what Frog's sewn body should look like now. More or less.

16. Carefully trim the seam allowances, and turn him. If you thought turning the arms was tedious, this might well take hours. Remember your training, Luke! The Force is with you, but only if you don't force the kebab stick.

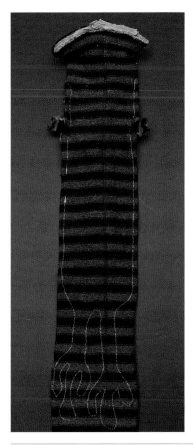

17. Now things get interesting. That's a diplomatic way of saying weird. We're going to use small empty spools and plenty of pipe cleaners to fashion Frog a pair of scaffolds for his legs.

18. Let's start with the pipe cleaners for his toes. Bend them into loops, one for each toe.

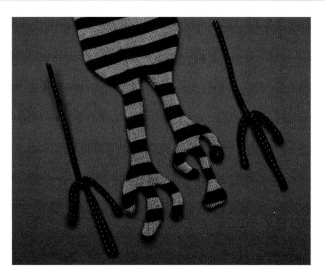

19. Stack 3 or 4 small spools (½" × ⅝"/1.25 cm × 1.5 cm; ⁷⁄₃₂"/.5 cm hole) onto each pipe-cleaner leg. Connect the 2 legs together by twisting the wire ends.

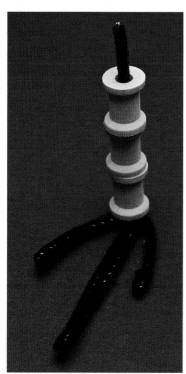

20. Begin working the scaffolding into Frog's body through the hole in his side.

21. Ease the scaffolding in place, fitting it into each toe and standing it upright. This may not be enough for Frog to stand on his own, but it will give him some help.

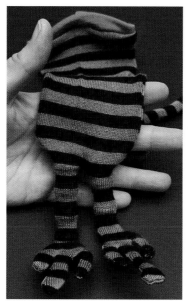

22. Stuff the rest of Frog's body, and seal up the opening in his side.

23. Now, he'll be wanting a pair of eyes. No seed beads for this dude. Look for large buttons or glass beads. Try to find something that has a strong color that will play off his lips or body.

Frog Lineup

"Kiss me, you fool!"

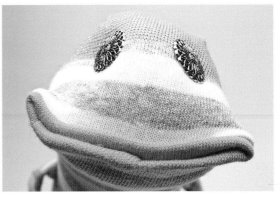

"Don't hate me because I am beautiful."

"Has anyone seen my chapstick?"

"That fly I just ate was *this* big!"

...and things that won't

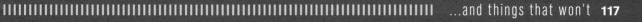

Designed and made by Brenna Maloney.

monster

Finished size: About 10″ (25.5 cm) tall

Monsters. Those things under the bed. Or in the closet. Or down the hall. They are out there and you are huddled in bed, always with your flashlight...just...out...of...reach! It was always the things you couldn't see that scared the pants off you. When you get older, your "unknowns" get scarier. You're up listening for burglars or the sounds of your children sleeping peacefully. And the things that scare you are not the things you can't see but the things you can't predict. The monsters grow. So, I wanted to make a sock creature that conveyed all that. Something that reflected the worry and panic we sometimes feel as grownups. And...I ended up failing miserably, of course. My monster isn't one bit scary. Even though I gave him fierce jiggity-jaggety teeth and mismatched limbs, he's...yeah...cute. Pathetic, isn't it? Well, maybe you can channel your inner demons better than I and come up with something that actually passes for a monster. In the meantime, I'll walk you through this cheerful mess.

instructions

1. Find yourself a pair of black knee-highs or thigh-highs. Root around in your Triple S (page 9) and find scraps or odd/single socks to make Monster's feet, his teeth, and the hoody-boos on the top of his head. Yeah, that's the technical term for them. You'll need a longer scrap for his arms. I used a lovely red knee-high. Mix things up here, in terms of color. As you can see, I've got quite a mix.

2. Cut the foot sections off both knee-highs, and remove the cuffs from the sock tops.

3. Slice the long sections open along the sides. Using my pattern (page 125) (or, better yet, creating a base shape of your own), cut out Monster's front and back body.

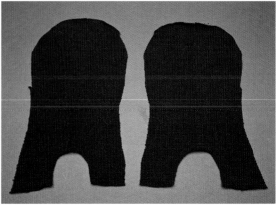

4. For the arms, use the long scraps or cut a length of the sock you chose. How long do you want these arms? I've no idea. Don't you know I'm making this up as I go along? Just make them, you know, longish. Think: knuckle dragger.

5. Free-sew yourself this pair o' arms. Here again, there are no rules. This is all you. I made 2 skinny tubes with 2 fingers at the end. Trim the seam allowances, turn, and set aside.

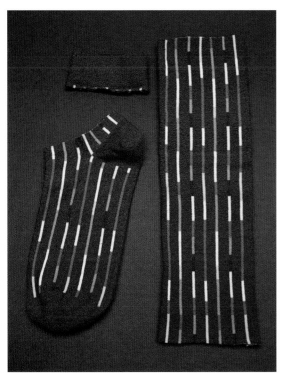

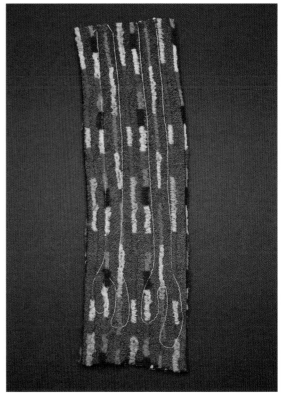

6. Find another bit of scrap. I'm using an orange anklet. Sew a jiggity-jaggety. Yes, you heard me. A jiggety-jaggety little whatsit that will become Monster's teeth. Okay, okay, I know I'm not speaking English. Just look at the picture and that should help. Make them fierce and pointy. Trim the seam allowances, turn, and set aside.

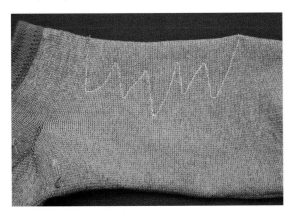

7. Find yourself another bit of scrap. Monster needs himself some toes. I've sewn 2 pointy sets of toes on a green anklet. Trim the seam allowances, turn, and set aside.

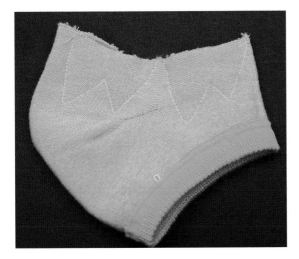

8. Find 2 more pieces of scrap—preferably non-matching pieces—and sew 2 skinny little tubes. These tubes will be the hoody-boos that go on his head. Oh, yeah. All monsters have these. Seriously. Trim the seam allowances and, well, you know the drill.

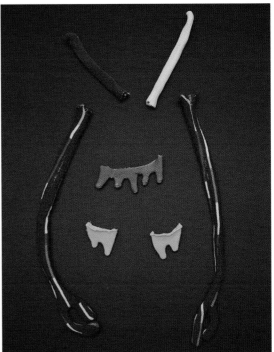

9. Grab a little segment of pipe cleaner, and insert it into each hoody-boo. After you've sewn them into his head, you're going to wrap the hoody-boos around a pencil to give them a curl or spiral shape. Don't do the wrapping now, though. I'm only hinting at what's up ahead. That's called "foreshadowing" in the literary world—a hint of what's to come to keep up the suspense. I'm on the edge of my seat. Aren't you?

10. Let's stitch the teeth to the body front. Set your machine to a satin stitch. (You might want to practice this stitch on a piece of scrap and make adjustments first.) You really want the stitch to cover the open edge of the teeth as well as create a line, almost like an upper lip. You can use matching thread or something contrasting. Up to you. Be brave! Be bold! Hey. Wait a second. Why are you hiding under your sewing table? Get out here this instant. I know the teeth are jiggity-jaggety, but really, YOU created them. You can't possibly be scared of them. What am I going to do with you?

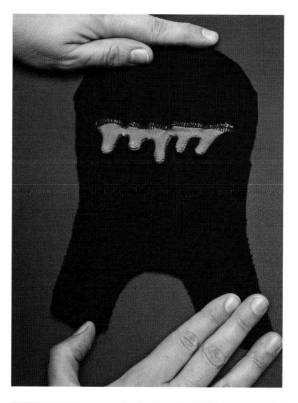

11. Lay the front half of Monster's body faceup. Position his arms, toes, and hoody-boos on top, all pointing inward, toward the center of his body. You'll have to almost ball up those arms in the center because they are so long.

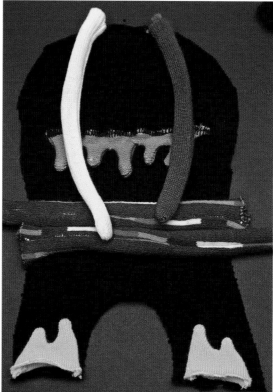

12. Place Monster's back body on the front body with right sides together, and pin, pin, pin. You want to trap everything in place. Carefully stitch around the body (don't hit any pins!). Remember to leave a small opening for turning.

13. Turn that sucker! Looking pretty cool now, huh?

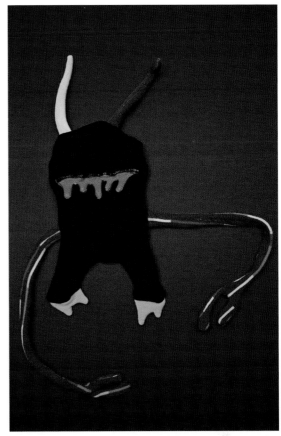

14. Gently stuff him—not too much—and stitch up the opening. You can get out that pencil now and spiral the hoody-boos. For the eyes, you can get pretty crazy. I chose these small buttons stitched on top of paper daisies. Weird, huh?

He's all set to terrorize.

Monster Improv Theater

I've given you a basic monster pattern, and I've already admitted that he's kind of lame in the scare department. Where you take it from here is up to you. As I said earlier, you can make up your own monster. I was more than a little disappointed in my own lameness, so I asked my sons to draw a few monsters for me as guides. Mine aren't exact matches, but…

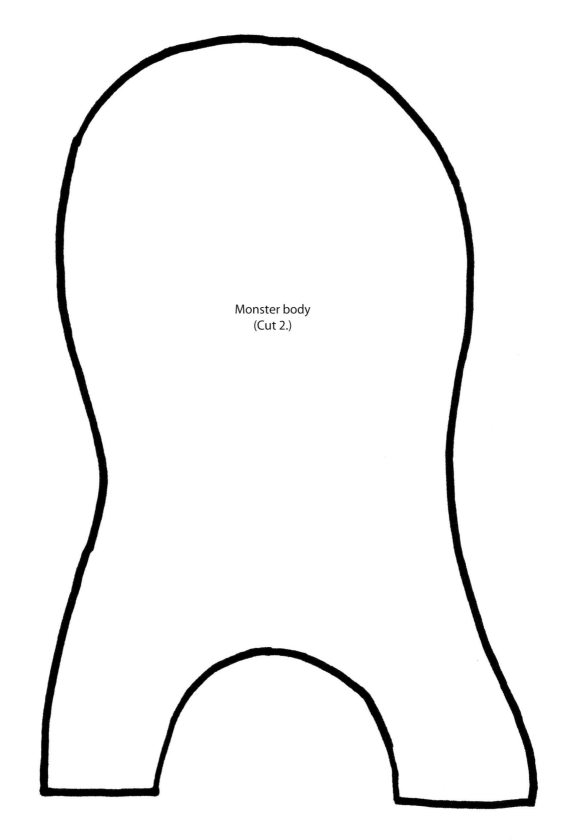

Monster body
(Cut 2.)

Designed and made by Brenna Maloney.

alien

Yeah. This is an alien wearing a jumpsuit. Why? I dunno. All the old science fiction books and movies have the human explorers wearing jumpsuits and the aliens are always naked. And you know, you feel kinda bad for the alien. He's standing around with his parts exposed to God and everyone and, well, maybe he's cold, right? Maybe he's freezing his doodley-doos off. Maybe *he'd* rather be wearing the jumpsuit while the humans prance around naked. So, we'll give him a jumpsuit, complete with belt buckle.

instructions

1. I like to make Alien's jumpsuit out of a gray sock, but you don't have to. Whatever color you choose, be sure to use a long sock, like a thigh-high. Or you can substitute 2 knee-highs. You'll also need a pair of colored anklets and some black scraps from your Triple S (or another anklet, black). The colored anklets are for his head and hands. Here, I've chosen red.

2. Cut the big ol' gray sock into several segments. The trick to this pattern is thinking in strips. Snip off the cuff, and cut a 3″ (7.5 cm), a 4″ (10 cm), and a 2½″ (6.25 cm) segment from whatever is left. Now you have an odd collection of little sock tubelets.

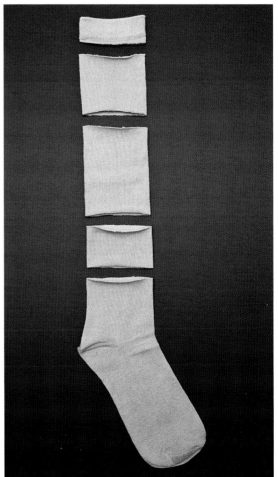

3. While you're in the mood for snipping, cut a 1″ (2.5 cm) segment from the black anklet (or black scrap).

4. Cut open the sides of the 3″ (7.5 cm) and 4″ (10 cm) gray segments and the 1″ (2.5 cm) black segment. Open them out flat.

5. Stitch these strips together to create 1 gray–black–gray strip set. You've just created Alien's chest, belt, and legs.

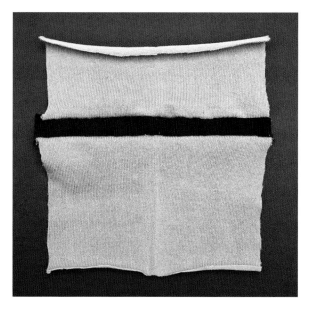

6. From 1 colored anklet, cut a 1″ (2.5 cm) segment. Split it down the side. Now, remember that 2½″ (6.25 cm) segment of gray I had you cut? Split that open next. Lay it alongside the red strip. Sew the red and gray pieces together. This will form Alien's arms and hannies.

> ### note
> I recently learned that "hannie" is not actually a word. When I use that word, I am referring, of course, to "hands." Growing up, everyone in my family always used this word when they meant "hands." Don't ask me where it came from; I have no idea. But I'm too old to change, so you'll just have to endure another word from Brennaspeak.

7. Now the fun begins! Fold the red and gray strip in half, end to end. Free-sew 2 arm/hannie combos. You can make these any way you like. Mine have 2 little pointies that will be Alien's fingers. Yeah, he only gets 2 on each hannie. But, don't forget, we're giving him a jumpsuit, so that makes up for everything. Trim away the excess.

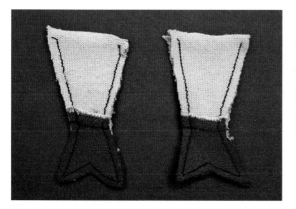

8. Find the other red anklet now. We're going to free-sew his head through the double thickness. You can follow my pattern (page 133) if you like, but you don't have to. You've probably seen enough science fiction flicks to help you picture what a good alien head might look like. I made mine a little pointy on the sides and gave him 3 doodley-doos in the middle. These will be eyestalks. You might want to draw up a few sketches before you start sewing. Then sew very slowly and carefully, to keep it all looking fairly even. Trim away the excess.

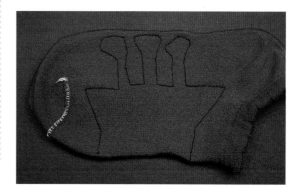

9. If you've given your alien eyestalks, turning his head will be no picnic. Just work very slowly, and try using the kebab stick to poke the eyestalks free. But don't get violent with your poking, or you'll poke a hole clean through.

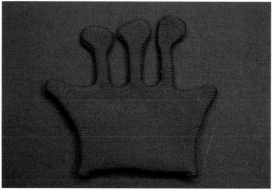

10. If you survived that, you can turn his arms next. He's looking pretty cool now, huh?

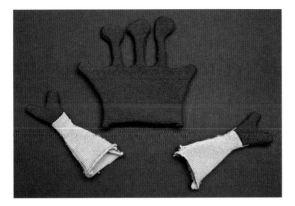

11. Now we're going to work on his body. Remember that gray–black–gray strip set from Step 5? Fold that in half, with right sides together. Slit open the folded edge of this sandwich to make a top and a bottom body. Slip the turned arms inside, just above Alien's belt. Pin them in place.

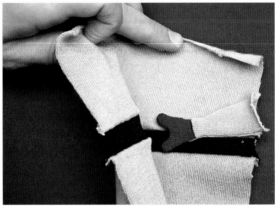

12. Starting at the neck, sew a line down to the first arm. We're going to give Alien a bit of a pear shape. (He actually eats pretty well on his planet, and he's not afraid if his jumpsuit bulges a bit here and there.) As you sew past his black waistband, start to curve in a bit. Just before you hit the bottom of the gray strip, free-sew a short leg and a foot. Well, give him 2, actually, separated by a small V-shaped gap. Continue to sew up until you reach the other side of the neck. Leave the neck open. Trim the seam allowance.

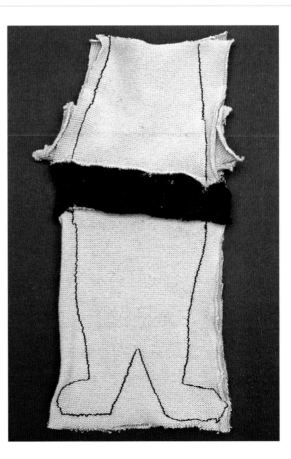

13. Now you're ready to attach Alien's head to his body. I know I told you to turn the head, but I need you to partially re-turn him by stuffing his eyestalks back into his head.

14. Pin together the head and neck most of the way around, right sides together, with raw edges lined up. Leave a small opening through which to turn him. Stitch carefully by hand or machine along his neck to attach the head to the body.

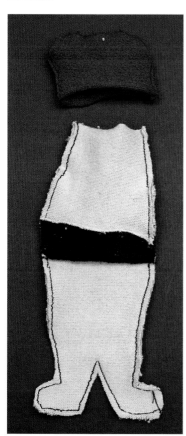

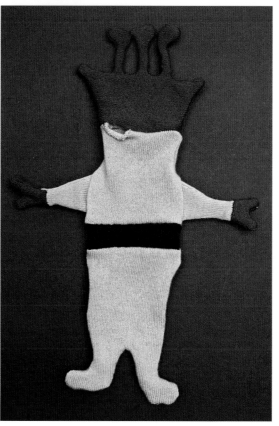

15. Turn Alien right side out. He looks like a limp noodle, but we're getting there.

16. Plump him up with some polyfill. Give him a nice round tum. Then, with a needle and matching thread, stitch up his neck opening.

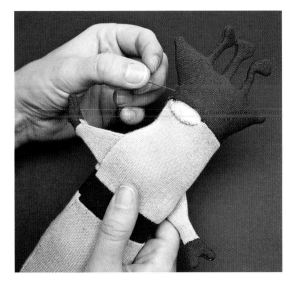

17. You can use whatever you like for eyes. I just hot glued wiggle eyes onto his eyestalks, burning my fingers, of course, in the process. I've never used that blasted glue gun without singeing something. Find yourself a little black DMC floss, 2 or 3 strands, and backstitch a wide smile on his face.

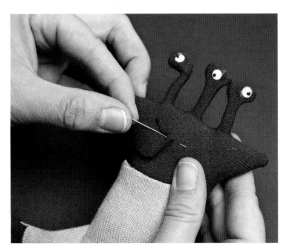

Now give him a big ol' belt buckle. It doesn't have to be Elvis-style—when Elvis squeezed himself into those double-knit polyester jumpsuits with the collars that consumed his head. No. It doesn't have to be *that* big. But go for something unique. I've tried large beads, buttons, even brads. Almost anything works. He's ready for human contact!

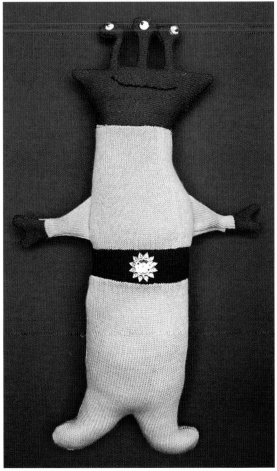

"Take me to your leader."

"I'm not sure this planet agrees with me."

"Does this jumpsuit make me look fat?"

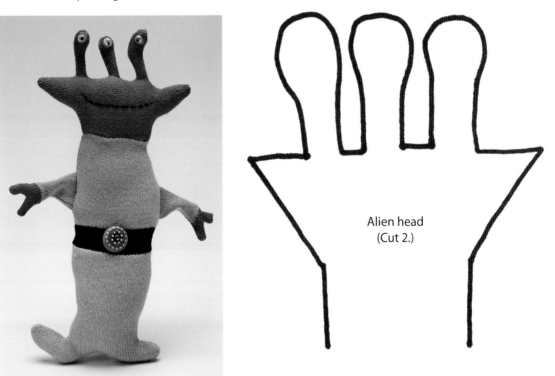

"Do you have Junior Mints on this planet?"

Alien head
(Cut 2.)

Designed and made by Brenna Maloney.

robot

Finished size: About 8″ (20 cm) tall

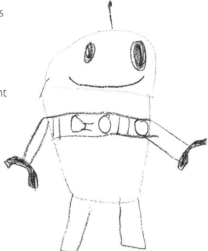

I might have mentioned to you that I have boys. My sons are ages 5 and 7. If you have boys or even know boys or have ever seen boys, you will know that boys have no patience for "girl things." And they aren't likely going to tolerate their mom spending all her hours in the basement sewing up sweet little mermaids or princesses. They want something interesting. They want something that matters. What they want are robots.

To make a truly impressive 'bot, it helps to seek advice from robot experts. Mine provided numerous sketches and countless pieces of useful advice (like, "More gears and springs, Mom, so he can jingle when he walks.").

instructions

1. For this robot, we need something sparkly! I found this fantastic black knee-high with gold sparkles.

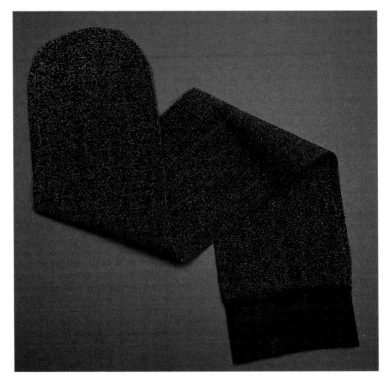

2. Lay the sock flat, cut off about 2″ (5 cm) of the toe section, and cut a 2″ (5 cm) sock segment.

3. Cut both layers of the 2″ (5 cm) sock segment into 3 parts. The middle piece will be the front and back of Robot's boxy head; the end pieces will be the sides of the head.

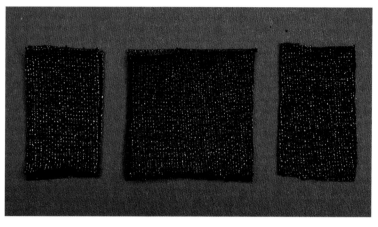

4. Separate the small end pieces, and lay them out as shown. They will become the sides, top, and bottom of the head box.

5. To make a faceplate for Robot, find a scrap of some type of shiny fabric. You'll also need a little piece of Pellon Wonder Under—a double-sided, paper-backed fusible web that you iron onto fabric. Press the Wonder Under to the shiny fabric (refer to the instructions for Sheep, page 62). Let it cool.

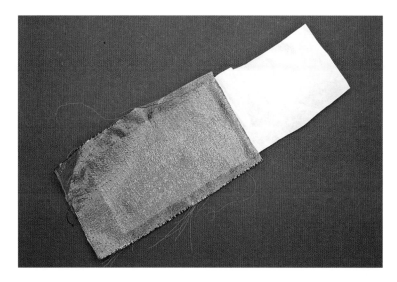

6. Sew together 4 of the head box pieces—the front, the back, and 2 of the sides—end to end.

7. Cut a small square of the shiny Pellon-backed fabric. It should be small enough to fit the face of Robot. Iron it in place. To make sure the fabric will hold, zigzag stitch it to Robot's face.

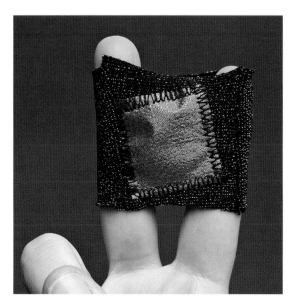

8. Sew the top onto the box by hand or machine, with right sides together and raw edges matching.

9. Add the bottom to the box, remembering to leave a small hole for turning.

10. Repeat this entire process to make a bigger box for Robot's body. Use a 4″ (10 cm) segment of sock this time, and repeat Steps 3 through 9.

11. Gently stuff both boxes, and stitch their openings closed.

12. With what's left of the sock, we'll make 2 large legs and also cut circles for the bottoms of Robot's feet. We'll use that very last little piece to create 2 skinny arms, and then we are out of sock! (If this is *really* a problem, just use the other sock.)

13. Each leg is essentially a large tube that will have a bottom sewn to it.

14. Eyeball the bottom as you cut it, to make sure it fits, and hand stitch it in place.

15. We want to give Robot stability, so we are going to stuff his feet with empty wooden spools.

16. Sew 2 skinny tubes for arms, and lightly stuff them.

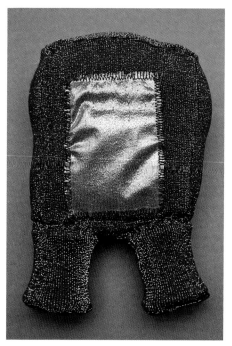

17. Using a slip stitch, sew the spool legs to Robot's body. Attach his head and arms in the same way.

Now, do nothing. Take a long break. He's done, but he's not "done." And what happens next may take some figuring out. Our next step is to embellish him. For this, you'll need robot "parts." Try all kinds of weird stuff—beads, wire, old watch parts, computer chips, bits from smashed cell phones or other electronics, springs, weird things you find in your kids' pockets when you're doing the laundry. Composing Robot's face and chest plate may take time. You might have to "audition" parts to see if they look good together. Here's what I came up with for this fella, but there are obviously many ways to do this. If you aren't sure which way to go with it, ask a child. Children always seem to know just what to do.

"I might need an upgrade. I'm feeling a little wonky."

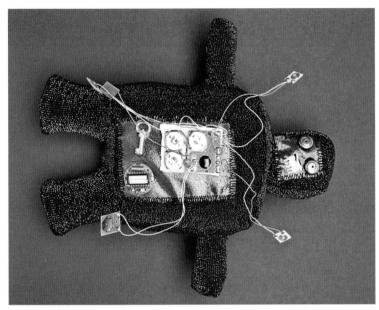

"Oh! My goodness! What are my innards doing on the outside?"

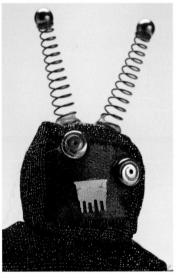

"I'll be back."

"Hey guys! Try holding your arms out like this. Your balance will be much better."

on the web

Guess what? I have a website! Well, who doesn't, you say. My eight-year-old cousin's sister's brother's chicken has a website. Maybe. But if you knew how technologically inept I am, you'd be cheering for me right now. Anyway... seeing as how I *have* one...maybe you could, you know, stop by for a visit? Here is the address: www.socksappeal.org. And while you're there, we could have a little chat. You can email me: socksappeal@me.com. Instead of having to listen to me blather on endlessly, you can blather back! You can tell me stuff. Don't tell me too much stuff, though. I mean, be reasonable, okay? I'm not sure I can help with everything. And if it's cooking advice you need, well, don't even go there with me. But, if it is sock related, well, then, hey, sure! It'll be so fun! You MUST DO IT.

Are you convinced yet? No? Oh.

That's okay. I was prepared for that. I know how to *lure* you. My publisher told me the secret: Give them FREE stuff, and they will come. So, if you visit my website, I will give you ABSOLUTELY FREE a FREE sock pattern. You heard me: ABSOLUTELY FREE, with no obligation to buy the elaborate knife set or the can of spray-on hair.

I think you will actually like this pattern. It's one of my favorites. It's called a Worry Wort. A Worry Wort is the thing that you make from a sock to help you cope with all the worries you carry around with you. It is stuffed with rice, which helps give it character and shoulder your burdens at the same time.

"We're not worried. Much."

final thoughts

Well, we've blazed through another set of patterns. A pleasure, my friend. I'm proud of you. You really put yourself out there a time or two. I know it's scary to take risks, but the reward can be great when you do it.

As always, I'm grateful that you spent time with me. Thanks for using this book. You know I'd like to hear from you and see your projects, so get on my website or drop me an email.

I'm going to head back into my sewing lair for a bit. I have a few new ideas...

Until next time,

Brenna

about the author

Brenna Maloney is the author of *Socks Appeal*. She lives with her husband and sons in Washington, D.C. You can find her at www.socksappeal.org and socksappeal@me.com.

Also by Brenna Maloney

Also available as an eBook